CALVINUS

Authentic Calvinism
A Clarification

Alan C. Clifford

Charenton Reformed Publishing

© Alan C Clifford 1996, 2007

First published in Great Britain 1996
by Charenton Reformed Publishing
www.christiancharenton.co.uk

New edition 2007

Typeset in Sabon and printed by Barkers Print & Design Ltd,
Attleborough, Norfolk NR17 2NP

British Library Cataloguing in Publication Data.
A catalogue record for this book is available from the British Library.

Cover concept (including the original 19th century Calvin Translation Society and
Norwich Reformed Church/Charenton Reformed Publishing logos):
the Author, executed by Barkers Print & Design Ltd

NRC/CRP logo development by David Fox

ON THE EVE OF THE CALVIN QUINCENTENARY

To

the memories

of

JOHN CALVIN
(1509-64)
'Calvin...knew more about the gospel
than almost any man who has ever lived, uninspired'
(C. H. Spurgeon)

and two of his
illustrious 'sons'

MOISE AMYRAUT
(1596-1664)

and

ANTOINE COURT
(1696-1760)

and the members of the
AMYRALDIAN ASSOCIATION

SOLI DEO GLORIA

Contents

Illustrations

Preface to the First Edition

For most Calvinists, the doctrine of limited atonement is axiomatic. Therefore any discussion which calls it into question, thereby weakening the apparent cohesion of the 'five points of Calvinism', is viewed with suspicion. However, the post-war revival of interest in Calvinism has inevitably renewed past debates about its precise character. Waverers who feel more at home with their Bibles than with systematic theologies are usually referred to such classical works as John Owen's *Death of Death* (1647), John Gill's *Body of Divinity* (1796) or William Rushton's *Defence of Particular Redemption* (1831).

While several members of the Westminster Assembly and other famous puritans and evangelicals such as Richard Baxter (1615-1691), Isaac Watts (1674-1748), Philip Doddridge (1702-1751), John Newton (1725-1807), Thomas Chalmers (1780-1847), Ralph Wardlaw (1779-1853) and J. C. Ryle (1816-1900) - to name but a few - are well known for teaching 'four point Calvinism', considerable attention has been focussed in recent decades on John Calvin (1509-1564) whose name, on account of his unique genius and contribution, is forever associated with the popular label for Reformed theology. In the wake of a 'moderate Calvinist' tradition which sees major discrepancies between Calvin and later Calvinists, Paul van Buren's *Christ in our Place* (1957), Brian G. Armstrong's *Calvinism and the Amyraut Heresy* (1969) and *R. T. Kendall's Calvin and English Calvinism to 1649* (1979) have discussed Calvin's views in some depth. These and other scholars have concluded that Calvin's theology was subsequently distorted by questionable scholastic influences.

Whether or not Calvin held to limited atonement is a question which continues to divide opinion, sometimes in very heated terms. For some, it is of little consequence what Calvin taught. In their view, limited atonement is the obvious teaching of the Bible - though others disagree! For those who feel the importance of theological tradition, it is a point of considerable embarrassment if Calvin did not teach a central tenet of their system. One response is to suggest that Calvin - dying forty years before the Arminian controversies of the early 17th century - never formally addressed the issue, in which case, precision is not to be expected in his writings. That said, some scholars believe that Calvin's utterances are 'consistent' with the formulated limited atonement doctrine of a later period. Others have endeavoured to prove that Calvin clearly embraced limited atonement, arguing that the reformer could hardly represent a deviant view within a tradition stretching from the age of Augustine of Hippo (354-430) to the present time.

Sympathising with those who believe that no one theologian in the Reformed tradition - not even Calvin - should determine our biblical understanding, CALVINUS is published with the conviction not only that conventional Calvinism continues to misread Calvin but that the great reformer - together with his true disciples - expresses for the most part the authentic teaching of Holy Scripture on this fundamental subject. It is hoped that these two issues will now be settled once and for all, to the glory of God and the growing effectiveness of evangelising Christians.

Dr Alan C. Clifford
Attleborough, Norfolk
1995

Preface to the Second Edition

More than a decade since it was first published and a couple of years since it went out of print, continuing demand seems to warrant a new edition of *Calvinus*. Well received by all but the most ardent disciples of John Owen (see review extracts, p. 64), this edition reflects continuing interest in a subject which shows no signs of subsiding. Partly to economise on space, a new Appendix III replaces the third and fourth originals. Changes have also been made to the illustrations. Since the first Appendix IV dealt with Calvin's view of Justification, I would refer the reader to a fuller treatment found in my *Atonement and Justification: English Evangelical Theology 1640-1790 - An Evaluation* (Clarendon: Oxford, 1990 rep. 2002). The new Appendix III is a response both to the Revd Iain H. Murray's 1996 review of *Calvinus* and his recent book *The Old Evangelicalism: Old Truths for a New Awakening* (Banner of Truth Trust, 2005). The discussion also takes account of another work of related significance from the same publisher *The Atonement Controversy in Welsh Theological* Literature and Debate, 1707-1841 by Owen Thomas, tr. by John Aaron (2002).

Since *Calvinus* first appeared, I have contributed other items relating to the atonement, mostly published by Charenton Reformed Publishing. These include *Sons of Calvin: Three Huguenot Pastors* (1999), *The Good Doctor: Philip Doddridge of Northampton, A Tercentenary Tribute* (2002), *Amyraut Affirmed* (2004), *Spotlight on Scholastics* (2005), *A Window on Welsh Calvinism* (2006), *A Quick Look at Amyraut* (Amyraldian Association Conference, 2006) and 'Introduction' to John Davenant's *Dissertation on the Death of Christ* (Quinta Press, 2006). Besides the Revd Iain Murray, this updated edition of *Calvinus* includes references to other scholars such as Professor Paul Helm (pp. 52, 56), Dr Richard Muller (p. 44), Dr Carl Trueman (p. 60) and Dr Garry Williams (p. 60).

As a theological writer with evangelistic and pastoral concerns, I am ever mindful of the sacred nature of the subject treated here. Convinced that - considerations of sovereign electing love apart - John Calvin would have happily sung the universal atonement hymns of Charles Wesley (1707-88), I believe it is entirely appropriate in this tercentenary year to conclude this preface with one of Wesley's hymns (still found in many hymn-books):

O LOVE divine! what hast Thou done?
The immortal God hath died for me!
The Father's co-eternal Son
Bore all my sins upon the tree;
The immortal God for me hath died!
My Lord, my Love is crucified.

2 Is crucified for me and you,
To bring us rebels back to God:
Believe, believe the record true,
Ye all are bought with Jesu's blood,
Pardon for all flows from His side;
My Lord, my Love is crucified.

3 Then let us sit beneath His cross,
And gladly catch the healing stream,
All things for Him account but loss,
And give up all our hearts to Him;
Of nothing think, or speak beside,
My Lord, my Love is crucified.

Dr Alan C. Clifford
Attleborough, Norfolk
February, 2007

Introduction

I

As his writings make abundantly clear, the great reformer John Calvin taught a doctrine of the atonement significantly different from that of later Calvinists. Indeed, he would hardly recognise the theory of limited atonement as his offspring. The key to understanding Calvin's very different view of the extent and efficacy of Christ's death is his view of the divine will. While Calvin believed God's will to be one, he insists that it is set before us in Scripture as double - secret and revealed (see quotations #21, 27, 73, 83). Conscious of its rational incomprehensibility (yet no more problematic than the doctrine of the Trinity), Calvin argued for this divine dichotomy from Deut. 29:29 and elsewhere.[1] As it relates to redemption, God's revealed will is universal and conditional but the secret will or counsel is restricted and absolute (#22, 74). While predestination and election relate to the latter, Calvin usually relates the Gospel to the former (#49, 81). Hence the death of Christ is presented by Calvin as universal according to God's revealed intention or decree, but limited in efficacy according to God's secret decree (#31, 42, 58, 63, 80). In his biblical comments, without speculating on any temporal or logical priority in the decrees, Calvin seems to stress one or the other according to strictly contextual considerations.

Accepting the delicate balance of this acute antinomy, it is truly remarkable that one who has been condemned for severe logicality should embrace a concept branded by its detractors as illogical. Yet Calvin insisted that humility of mind is demanded in the face of transcendent truth. After his death, his finely tuned biblical balance was effectively destroyed by the ultra-orthodoxy of Theodore Beza (1519-1605) and the reactionary sub-orthodoxy of Jakob Arminius (1560-1609). Their theological antagonism notwithstanding, they agreed on the priority of strict rational consistency. Thus the two strands in Calvin's composite thought were separated with unhappy soteriological results. While Beza insisted on an atonement limited by decree, design and efficacy, Arminius - denying divine foreordination - taught an unlimited, hypothetical atonement. Thus the two sides of a supra-logical, paradoxical coin were rent asunder. The opposing positions were alike rationalistic; theologians adjusted and modified textual evidence which conflicted with their particular perspective. Whereas the Arminians made election conditional and God's redemptive purpose contingent, the high Calvinists squeezed the universal language of Scripture into a rigidly particularist mould. Calvin would have rejected this double-distortion of his theology. To be sure, Beza's marginal gloss on John 3:16 in the French Geneva Bible (1588) limiting the 'world' so loved by God to the elect involved a degree of textual tampering Calvin would have regarded as reprehensible.[2]

French Geneva Bible

High Calvinists have claimed that their restrictive exegesis of terms like 'world' and 'all' has a precedent in Calvin, especially in his exposition of 1 Timothy 2:4-6 (see #71). However, the case is unfounded, despite some similarity of language. Whereas the English high Calvinist John Owen (1616-83) treats the will of God in 1 Timothy 2 as the 'efficacious' or absolute will,[3] Calvin expounds it as the revealed, conditional will. *Failure to detect this has led high Calvinist expositors to misinterpret Calvin's thought.* True, Calvin and Owen agree that Paul is discussing racial and social groups rather than individuals, yet this means something totally different according to the underlying conception of the divine will assumed by each expositor. Indeed, their respective uses of this observation are diametrically opposed. While Owen expounds Paul's 'all' as 'elect individuals of all sorts', Calvin denies that the apostle has the elective, secret counsel of God in mind. In short, Calvin asserts that Paul is not speaking of elect 'individuals of nations' according to God's secret will but 'nations of individuals' (#72) invited to the Gospel according to God's revealed will. Thus when Calvin speaks of racial or social classes, he is not denying that the Gospel makes redemptive provision for individual members of each group: the 'each' in his comment on John 1:29 (#44) is clearly 'each individual', not 'each nation'. Thus Calvin does not use classification as a limiting factor as Owen does; on the contrary the atonement is unlimited since no class or 'nation of individuals' is excluded from 'the hope of salvation' according to the revealed preaching of the Gospel. On the other hand, Owen's exegesis would be valid if Paul had God's 'secret counsel' in view, but Calvin denies that this is the case. A careful reading of the evidence now presented will demonstrate the fundamental error of citing Calvin's exegesis as a precedent for the high orthodox view.

While several unrestricted atonement statements show no trace of any ambiguity (see especially #12, 54, 55, 68, 69, 79, 87), it is admitted that one or two of Calvin's textual and theological observations do not readily conform to his general view. Yet what seem like deviations from the rule are, on closer examination, more consistent with 'authentic' rather than high Calvinism. A case in point is Calvin's comment on 1 John 2:2 (#84). The seeming agreement in exegesis here between Calvin and Owen - that John writes of 'actual' as opposed to 'offered' salvation confined to the church throughout the whole world - is more than counterbalanced by the wider differences. Since Calvin was opposing the theory of an absolute universalism advanced by certain 'fanatics', even embracing the possible salvation of Satan as well as the reprobate, he did not resort to his usual exegetical formula. Calvin also admits here the truth of the sufficiency-efficiency distinction, only denying - surely unnecessarily, except where Satan is concerned - that it fits the passage. In Calvin's mind, the only issue here was the effectuality of the atonement, not its wider sufficiency. But his view of a universal propitiation (#20, 77) obviously distances him from Owen's basic approach to 1 John 2: 2.[4] Faced with textual abuse, Calvin's comments clearly reflect concern with the application of the atonement rather than its universal provision for sinful humanity. What he certainly does not say is that 'whole world' means the 'elect world'. Combining #84 with the thrust of #85, by definition no salvation is applied to the reprobate, *qua* reprobate, i.e. viewing such individuals from the standpoint of the secret decree. Calvin's note here on Jn 11:52 assumes that perspective: Christ's office is only to *gather* (or *grasp* (#83) or *effectually* redeem) the elect. What is remarkable is that he still maintains in #85 a universal expiation of sin and the consequent offer of reconciliation to all, including the reprobate *qua* 'poor sinners' - as he describes 'all' elsewhere (#42, 43, 90). In short, notwithstanding the secret will's guarantee of the salvation of the elect, the revealed will makes salvation available to all.

Another passage from the *Treatise on Predestination* (#63) appears to suggest that an otherwise universal atonement was merely designed to save the elect. Thus high Calvinists have sought to particularize Calvin's universalist language. They fail to see that again Calvin is mainly discussing the *efficacy* of redemption in the light of God's secret counsel. Calvin obviously taught that the elect partake efficaciously of an atonement nonetheless provided for all conditionally. Indeed, while stressing this point, he still specifically says: 'That it is salvific for all I do not deny' and 'the same mediator is set forth for all to reconcile them to the Father'. It is important therefore not to do violence to Calvin's ubiquitous universalism in the interests of a misplaced particularism. When his statements are particularist, he is merely affirming the certain and limited efficacy of redemption in

Calvin opposing universalism of Scripture

Calvin's absolute salvation

Theory of

the case of the elect, rather than denying an ordained salvific universalism which undergirds the proclamation of the Gospel. When Calvin speaks of God saving the elect, he is merely stating the undeniable, but he nowhere employs the exclusive particularist expression 'Christ died only for the elect'. Without questioning that Calvin often speaks of the efficacious redemption of the church, it is equally beyond doubt that he affirms a conditional salvation for all (#22, 74).

In view of the perspicuity of Calvin's position, it is surprising how his isolated particularist statement against the Lutheran divine Heshusius has been exploited by high orthodox writers. Calvin says: 'As he adheres so doggedly to the words ['this is my body'], I should like to know how the wicked can eat the flesh of Christ which was not crucified for them, and how they can drink the blood which was not shed to expiate their sins?'[5] Once it is seen - judging by the opening words of the statement - that Calvin is opposing the Lutheran theory of consubstantiation, an otherwise problematic statement makes sense beside his numerous univeralist statements. He is virtually asking how unbelievers (or anyone else for that matter) can feed on a crucified Christ simply by eating and drinking consecrated elements; for they themselves were not actually crucified as Christ was. Calvin is simply ridiculing the idea that unbelievers feed on Christ by feeding on mere symbols.[6]

II

For all the opprobrium poured upon the French Amyraldians by high orthodox theologians, the Calvin material cited below was the basis of that authentic Calvinism claimed by Moïse Amyraut (1596-1664) and many of his fellow theologians and pastors. Despite the angry assaults of the high orthodox party, the Amyraldians argued that they were simply perpetuating and reproducing Calvin's theology. Such were Amyraut's debating skills that condemnation of him was seen as a condemnation of Calvin! Repeated attempts to discipline Amyraut failed: between the years 1637 and 1659, three National Synods of the French Reformed Churches expressed confidence in his teaching.[7] To reinforce his claim to orthodoxy, Amyraut defended himself by utilising the phraseology of the *Canons of Dordt*![8] Many pastors and elders were in agreement with Amyraut. Among the leading preachers, Jean Daillé (1594-1670), pastor of the great temple at Charenton near Paris, is famous for his support.[9] He was joined by two of his pastoral colleagues at Charenton, Jean Mestrezat (1592-1657) and Michel Le Faucheur (c. 1595-1657). They considered that it would be absurd if no room was found in the Reformed churches of France for Calvin's type of theologizing.[10]

While their particular theological method derived from Calvin, the Amyraldians were dubbed as 'new methodists'. They placed biblical theology before systematic theology: thus dogmatics were to be derived from exegesis. On the evangelistic and pastoral level, the Amyraldians considered that the high orthodox alternative both prevented a candid exegesis of Scripture and inhibited evangelism. They believed that in the proclamation of the Gospel, initial stress should be placed on the revealed conditional will of God, the secret elective will of God then being introduced to assure believers of their salvation. This is precisely the order followed by Paul[11] in his Epistle to the Romans and Calvin in his *Institutes*. Predestination is thus regarded as an *ex post facto* explanation of why some believe and others do not. Despite common and persistent criticism of Amyraut's doctrine of predestination, he denied the charge of reversing the order of the divine decrees. Indeed, he emphatically refused to expatiate on the issue. Like Calvin, Amyraut regarded speculation about

9

See
note 12

matters not revealed in Scripture as vain and presumptuous curiosity. However, he believed there was a revealed order in the presentation of the biblical Gospel which Aristotle-inspired, scholastic orthodoxy had rejected.[12]

Without doubt, Amyraut, Professor of Theology at the Reformed Academy in Saumur was Calvin's theological heir, as F. P. Van Stam's interesting observations make clear:

> Amyraut...revealed the attraction which the theology of Calvin held for him. He demonstrated this preference in an array of books, in the process proving his familiarity with the writings of this reformer. If the fact that after 1617 (on the eve of the Synod of Dordt) the number of new editions of Calvin's *Institutes* declined is not an isolated, merely incidental phenomenon, then this suggests a change, if not a decrease, in interest in Calvin in that period. This could also imply that Amyraut rediscovered Calvin, as it were, and was perhaps the Calvin-expert of the day. In any case, Amyraut fell under the spell of Calvin's theology.[13]

Van Stam's work disproves beyond all doubt the propriety of that subtle suggestion that the Revocation of the Edict of Nantes (1685) was a divine judgement on the French Protestants for tolerating Amyraut's teaching,[14] and the less than subtle description of Amyraut as 'the grave digger'[15] of the French Reformed Church. To say in effect that a return to authentic Calvinism destroyed the Reformed churches of France is an opinion hardly worth mentioning, far less refuting.

That said, recent research confirms the absurdity of linking the supposed debilitation of French Calvinism to Amyraldianism.[16] Abjuration statistics give an entirely contrary picture, especially where the pastors were concerned. Since Amyraut's influence was greatest north of the Loire, it is a striking fact that pastors were generally more faithful in the northern provinces where 8 per cent abjured compared with 18 per cent in the 'high orthodox' southern provinces. In particular, the province of the Ile-de-France lost 4 per cent compared with 27 per cent in the Cévennes and 41 per cent in Béarn.[17] It is significant that in the north, unlike the south, the smaller protestant population owed its strength more to personal conviction than to nominal adherance.

Contrary to the fears of their high orthodox critics, the Amyraldian pastors still combined an eirenic spirit with a decided aversion to Roman Catholic dogma. If their Calvinism was kinder and less socially aggressive,[18] their theological commitment was unquestioned, even if, for various 'worldly-wise' reasons, apostasies were not uncommon among their adherents. To blame Amyraut for facilitating easy defections to Rome among the Reformed[19] is a travesty of truth. As famous as he was for a philanthropy without religious discrimination, his fidelity to the Reformed Faith was evident to the last. Indeed, John Quick's account of Amyraut's death-bed utterances put the matter beyond all doubt:

> [He proved] the truth of the Christian religion, and of our Holy Reformed religion, by many unanswerable arguments. "This I have professed," said he; "I have preached this Holy Reformed religion well nigh forty years." And turning himself unto the Papists (for there were many then present in his chamber, spectators and witnesses of his last end) "Gentlemen," said he, "This is the only true religion, and out of it there is no salvation. That God to whom I am going knows that I do speak the very truth." This, and much more he uttered with a clear and audible voice; yea, and those very Papists heard him with much reverence and attention.[20]

Indeed, none can doubt the protestant credentials of the author of *Brief Traitté de la Predestination* (1634) and *Defense de la doctrine de Calvin* (1644), a verdict no less applicable to Jean Daillé[21] and also to Jean Claude (1619-87), one of the last of Charenton's eminent pastors.[22]

A relatively recent popular evaluation of Claude may be regarded as typical of the misinformation used to blacken the Amyraldians. F. Orna-Ornstein, after suggesting that the preachers of the revocation period had ceased 'to glory in the great evangelical truths',[23] accuses Claude of neglecting the priority of evangelistic preaching in his *Essay on the Composition of a Sermon*.[24] Indeed, we are told that 'The conversion of sinners is passed over in silence.'[25] However, the falsehood of this observation is easily refuted by the very work thus maligned. Judging by his eulogy on the converting power of the gospel and a moving Amyraldian account of the dying thief[26] Claude is clearly vindicated on both counts. Comparing this with Calvin's explicit statements (#39, 42), Claude is as worthy a disciple of the reformer as Amyraut had been a generation earlier. Thus Orna-Ornstein's questionable characterization of Amyraldianism as a heterodox blend of Calvinism and Arminianism[27] implicates Calvin quite as much as his authentic disciples.

In a more scholarly but equally prejudiced vein, J-M Berthoud subjects Amyraut to scathing criticism. We are told that the 'doctrinal solidity' demanded of ministerial candidates by the Genevan Company of Pastors would, in the next century, 'stick in the throat of Amyraut'.[28] So, for all his criticism of Bezan high orthodoxy, are we to imagine that Amyraut's Alençon statement is dishonest rhetoric? Amyraut, together with his 'fellow heretic' Paul Testard of Blois (1599-1650), declared that 'it was never in their thoughts to propound or teach any doctrine whatever, but what was agreeable to the known and common expositions of our Creed, and contained in our Confession of Faith, and in the Decisions of the National Synod held at Charenton, in the year 1623; all which they were ready to sign with their best blood.'[29] Appealing to the 1559 *Confessio fidei Gallicana* (or the *Confession of La Rochelle*, 1571) - which Calvin helped to draw up - and the Canons of Dordt thus embraced by the French Reformed Churches in 1623, suggests a 'doctrinal solidity' Calvin would have rejoiced to see in his 'pupil' Amyraut! Furthermore, for Berthoud to attempt to drive a wedge[30] between Calvin's and Amyraut's similar exegesis-based teaching is to forget that both 'master' and 'pupil' were alike seeking to rid theology of Aristotelian scholasticism, both Roman and Reformed![31]

Amyraut's clear commitment to the *Canons of Dordt* suggests that the Amyraldians are the true 'five point' Calvinists. If anything, the high orthodox may be styled 'four and a half pointers', since they virtually deny the universal sufficiency of the atonement clearly expressed in the second canon. The conventional nomenclature really trades on an ignorance of what the canon actually says (see n. 8). Amyraut never called into question the restricted efficacy of the atonement. In short, the Amyraldians believed more than the high orthodox, not *less*.

Berthoud pursues his anti-Amyraldian polemic in his study of Claude Brousson (1647-98),[32] the ex-lawyer and 'desert pastor' who ministered with incomparable heroism to the persecuted churches in the immediate post-revocation period. As well as stating incorrectly - twice in fact - that Amyraut was moderator of the National Synod of Loudun (1659) - an honour, in fact, bestowed upon Daillé,[33] Berthoud fails to provide an exact portrayal of Brousson's position. Holding to a 'moderate high orthodox' Calvinism, Brousson's criticism of Amyraldian theology is thus distinctly mild compared with Berthoud's. Writing to the refugee pastors, Brousson warned against theological aberrations:

It is still this same spirit of novelty which gave place among us to the doctrine of universal grace. I believe that in France those who held this doctrine encompassed it within very narrow parameters. But we must be careful, my very honoured brothers, not to open the door to error...'[34]

Sharing precisely these same concerns earlier in the century, Amyraut, Daillé and others firmly denied the charge of novelty.[35] Endorsing Calvin's view against what they saw as high orthodox excesses, the Amyraldians vigorously defended a dualistic doctrine of universal and particular grace.[36] Indeed, to say that the controversy was only about 'universal grace' distorts their balanced concerns. From the opposite perspective, the French Arminian de Courcelles did not recognise Amyraut as an ally. Even he acknowledged that Amyraut's doctrine was the same as Calvin's.[37] Brousson's uneasiness regarding Amyraldianism thus reflects the usual high orthodox failure to grasp the full-orbed significance of Calvin's actual teaching. However, his federal theology places him closer to Amyraut than he perhaps realised. Whereas his English near-contemporary John Owen said that the covenant of grace 'was not made universally with all, but particularly only with some',[38] Brousson - though advocating limited atonement - declared:

It is true that the covenant of grace is beneficial to all men. But that can only mean that it is beneficial to those who repent and believe in the Gospel from any country in the world. That is why the Gospel is preached to all people...It is so that we can be led to love all men without distinction and to do all in our power to prevent them from perishing. But that does not mean that God absolutely wants the conversion of all men. For if he wanted to convert every single person he could do it...[39]

Judging by John Quick's evaluation of Amyraut's theology,[40] Brousson was closer to Amyraut and thus to Calvin than Berthoud imagines.

Turning lastly to 18th century developments in French Calvinism, high orthodox critical perspectives are again questionable. Henry Baird wrote that 'the churches of the desert developed an aversion to the strict Calvinism of the sixteenth century. This was evidenced by a marked preference for the catechism of the well-known Swiss theologian Jean Frédéric Ostervald (1663-1747)'.[41] Indeed, these changes were reflected in decisions made at the National Synod of 1744 and the Provincial Synod of Lower Languedoc of 1771 authorising the catechism's use among the churches. Significantly, this period includes the remarkable influence of Antoine Court (1696-1760). Nick-named in his youth 'Calvin's eldest son' by his Roman Catholic schoolmates, Court is regarded as the 'Huguenot Nehemiah'.[42] His astonishing ministry - commencing in 1715, the very year Louis XIV died - led to the revival and reorganisation of the Reformed churches in France. In his study of Court, Berthoud - never slow to repeat his criticism of Amyraut - goes further than Baird, lamenting the fact that Ostervald's catechism with its 'Arminian tendencies'[43] replaced the 'calvinist catechism' of Drelincourt. If Berthoud is correct, Court's theological leadership was arguably compromised, not least because of his prominent role in the 1744 synod. Indeed, since the Vivarais synod of 1721 had authorised the catechism of Charles Drelincourt (1595-1669)[44] - a colleague of Daillé's but a 'neutral' in the Amyraut controversy, this might imply a shift in Court's theology. If so, the anomaly is difficult to explain since Court, during his early 'desert' ministry and later labours in the Lausanne Academy, seems to have taught faithfully that famous symbol of French Calvinism, the *Confession of La Rochelle*.[45]

Several questions therefore demand an answer. What does Baird understand by 'the strict Calvinism of the 16th century'? The theology of Calvin's *Institutes*, commentaries and Genevan catechism, or

Beza's more developed orthodoxy? Or does he really mean the fully-mature high orthodoxy of Amyraut's 17th century opponents, Pierre du Moulin (1568-1658) and Frederick Spanheim (1600-49)?[46] And what of the supposed Arminian heterodoxy of Ostervald's catechism, approved by a national synod with the apparent complicity of Antoine Court?

Before Ostervald's catechism is examined, a brief glance at Pierre du Moulin is relevant. Berthoud states that Court's close associate Pierre Corteiz - through whom Court received ordination in 1718 - was 'nourished at the source of pure Calvinism by reading the writings of the celebrated Pierre du Moulin'.[47] Of course, all this is part of Berthoud's virulent denigration of the 'twisted' doctrines of Saumur.[48] However, while he cited the source of Brousson's mild criticism of Amyraut's views, he fails to identify the Du Moulin works Corteiz had read. The uncited list of pastoral and controversial works in his frequently quoted source[49] includes none of Du Moulin's specifically anti-Amyraldian treatises. Even here, Du Moulin's track record is not without ambiguity. Just as 'early' John Owen employed a typically 'Baxterian' view of common grace in his *Display of Arminianism* (1643),[50] so Du Moulin - the 'French Owen' - used remarkably 'proto-Amyraldian' language in his *Anatomy of Arminianism* (1619), written when Amyraut was only a student and published at the time of the Synod of Dordt! Du Moulin declared:

> When we say that Christ died for all men, we take it thus, that the death of Christ is sufficient to save all men, if all men in the whole world did believe in him: And that the cause why all men are not saved, is not in the insufficiency of the death of Christ, but in the wickedness and incredulity of man. Finally Christ may be said to reconcile all men to God by his death, after the same manner that we may say the sun doth enlighten the eyes of all men, though many are blind, many sleep, and many are hid in darkness'.[51]

Just as Owen was to delete 'common grace' from his *Death of Death* (1647), so Du Moulin's orthodoxy was to 'harden' by the time he opposed Amyraut fifteen years later. So, if Du Moulin's influence is relevant to Berthoud's anti-Amyraut thesis, he fails to demonstrate this in the case of Corteiz's theological development. Beside, at this early period, Court, Corteiz and their companions also read certain unspecified sermons by the Amyraldian Jean Claude.[52] No doubt it was the common protestant convictions of these authors which strengthened the youthful restorers of the French Reformed churches. To imagine that Claude was any less resolute than his high orthodox brethren is to ignore his *La Defense de la Reformation* (1673).

Comparing Ostervald's catechism (1702) with Drelincourt's (1642) alongside Calvin's Genevan catechism (1545) - bound up in French Protestant Bibles with 'La Forme des Priéres' and the 'Confession de Foi' late into the 17th century - helps to explain why Court's leadership was in no way compromised. Despite the intense theological activity of the intervening period, there are remarkable simlarities in detail and emphasis. The differences chiefly concern the level of anti-Roman rhetoric, a reflection of the circumstances of the times. Ostervald - and Calvin to a degree - wrote in the relative security of a protestant Swiss canton compared with the anti-protestant hostility constantly faced by Drelincourt and the Reformed churches in France. However, a real sense of theological continuity is evident, especially where 'Calvinist distinctives' are concerned.

Contrary to Berthoud's unsubstantiated remarks, an obvious feature of all three catechisms is the absence of any 'limited atonement' teaching. Predictably, Ostervald says that 'A Christian ought to believe that Jesus Christ is...the Saviour of the world; that He died for our sins, and that He has procured salvation and eternal life for all those that believe in Him'.[53] Perhaps surprisingly, Calvin showed no inhibitions in saying that 'Christ, who is the salvation of the world...expiated our sins before God, and so having appeased the wrath of God, restored [believers] to his favour' (#89).[54] Even more surprisingly, Drelincourt - when combatting Rome's multiple mediators - declares fully and without the least qualification: 'There is only one God, and one only mediator between God and men, the man Christ Jesus who gave himself a ransom for all, 1 Tim. 2, wherefore St John telleth us, in the second of his first Epistle, My little children...we have an advocate with the Father, Jesus Christ the righteous; and he is the propitiation for our sins, and not for ours only, but also for the sins of the whole world...'[55] So, if Ostervald's use of universalist language (albeit simply biblical, eg Jn. 4: 42) makes Berthoud suspicious, what is to be said of Calvin's and moreso of Drelincourt's? Whatever may be charged against Ostervald applies equally to the other two. To be sure, neither Ostervald nor Calvin nor Drelincourt equate 'the world' with 'the elect' nor is Christ's death described in restricted terms.

What then of election and predestination? Not surprisingly, Calvin describes the church as 'The body and society of believers predestined to eternal life'[56], 'the sons of God' by 'adoption and grace',[57] adding that 'All whom God has chosen he justifies'.[58] Similarly, Drelincourt - notwithstanding the extent of Christ's mediation - says that 'The word church....in its most excellent signification is taken for the company of those that God hath elected to life everlasting, whose names before the foundation of the world, he hath written in the Book of life...'[59] But with equally impeccable orthodoxy, Ostervald explains the meaning of 'adoption': 'That God, by an effect of his goodness, and for Jesus Christ's sake, has chosen us to be his children. Eph. 1: 4,5 *Having predestinated us unto the adoption of children by Jesus Christ to himself, according to the good pleasure of his will'.*[60] When expounding the Lord's Prayer ('Thy kingdom come') Calvin says that God 'governs the elect by his Spirit'.[61] Drelincourt describes 'the reign of grace' as 'That which Jesus Christ exercises on earth by his Spirit in his church, and in the hearts of his elect...'[62] Likewise, Ostervald states that God 'reigns...by his Spirit, over the hearts of his elect'.[63] Undoubtedly, all this looks solidly and healthily Calvinist! However, if Ostervald's Calvinism is deficient in Berthoud's eyes, it looks remarkably orthodox alongside Calvin's and Drelincourt's teaching. Indeed, one might say that Ostervald's theology represents a continuing expression of 'strict authentic Calvinism'. If anything, Drelincourt ought to arouse Berthoud's suspicions, for the Huguenot pastor explicitly teaches the two-fold will of God idea Amyraut derived from Calvin.[64]

If Berthoud wishes to penalize Ostervald for teaching that God 'permits sin'[65] (rather than 'ordaining it' by his 'secret counsel' - an 'evasion' Calvin might accuse him of,[66] if intended by the author - to the detriment of absolute divine sovereignty), it is surely significant that Calvin, though he argues against an abuse of the distinction in his *Institutes*, is happy to admit in his catechism that 'devils and wicked men....cannot do anything unless by [God's] permission'.[67] Of course, it is wrong to expect the precision of a systematic theology in a catechism chiefly intended for the young. In this respect, Calvin is rescued from the charge of contradiction and Ostervald from the charge of heterodoxy. Needless to say, all three theologians repudiate the notion that God's sovereignty makes him the author of sin.

The conclusion then is obvious. While 17th century high orthodoxy was a thing of the past, that is not the same as saying that a Calvinism closely approaching Calvin's and Amyraut's was not alive and well. After all, as Berthoud[68] and Orna-Ornstein[69] both indicate, Court had read in his boyhood a book by Richard Baxter (1615-91), famous for espousing Amyraldianism in 17th century

England.[70] Neither author identifies the Baxter work in question. However, Court himself reveals that it was *La voix de Dieu qui appelle les pécheurs à la repentance et à la conversion,*[71] famously known in the English-speaking world as the *Call to the Unconverted* (1658). The work appeared in several French editions. Court very possibly read the fifth edition, published rather appropriately at Saumur in 1680.[72] The obvious appetite for this publication surely challenges Orna-Ornstein's thesis that French Reformed spirituality was moribund at this period. In language which Calvin, Amyraut and, judging by his catechism, Drelincourt would have approved of, Court would have learned from Baxter that the death of Christ was not 'only for the elect. For it was...the sin of all the world that lay upon our redeemer; and his sacrifice and satisfaction is sufficient for all, and the fruits of it are offered to one as well as to another...'[73] In the absence of any hard evidence to the contrary (and Berthoud supplies none), such was very probably the character of Court's Calvinism. This is surely implied in Berthoud's heavily biassed criticism that Court's Lausanne Academy did not provide effective protection against Arminianism and Amyraldianism.[74] If such was the case, and high Calvinism did not appeal to him, it surely explains why Court saw nothing suspicious in Ostervald's theology.

A final relevant twist to our theological story introduces us to another Reformed catechism and offers surprising vindications of both Ostervald and Amyraut. It concerns one Etienne Gibert, 'the pious and earnest pastor of Bordeaux'.[75] Objecting to Ostervald's catechism, Gibert published a French edition of the *Heidelberg Catechism* without consulting his elders. Although it was affirmed that this famous Reformed symbol was 'approved among the Protestant communions in general',[76] Gibert was censured for the manner of his action by his provincial synod in September 1770. From Baird's and Berthoud's critical perspective, one might imagine that Gibert's preference was for a catechism more Calvinist than Ostervald's. However, this was not the case. Influenced as he was by Moravian pietism, doubts had been expressed about Gibert's Calvinstic orthodoxy. For instance, he questioned an excessive preoccupation with predestination in the pulpit and its consequent undermining of general gospel invitations. Significantly, Amyraut had expressed similar concerns a century before. However, unlike Ostervald's catechism, the Heidelberg makes no mention of either 'predestination' or 'election' in the text itself although God's sovereignty in providence and grace are clearly affirmed in equivalent terms with appropriate supporting 'proof texts'. In which case, Gibert quite possibly regarded Ostervald's catechism as too orthodox! However, it appears that there was more to Gibert's action than mere theological precision. Indeed, he was possibly attracted temperamentally to the warmth and beauty of the *Heidelberg Catechism* (1563)[77] rather than to the 'classical' lucidity of Ostervald's. That said, the post-scholasticism of Ostervald compares favourably with the pre-scholasticism of the earlier catechism, and there is little theologically to choose between them. Gibert, concerned that the Reformed doctrine of justification was being 'forgotten'[78] in the wake of a fashionable moralism, had no reason to doubt Ostervald's unambiguous teaching on that subject.[79] Significantly, Gibert had some support from Antoine Court's close friend and successor, the 'apostle of the desert' Paul Rabaut (1718-94).[80] It was during the period of the latter's leadership that the provincial synod of Lower Languedoc also approved Ostervald's catechism in 1771.

While it is doubtful whether Gibert was interested in the significance of the *Heidelberg Catechism* for a proper understanding of Calvin (for whom he had seemingly only a limited admiration), the controversy he sparked off serves to highlight the relevance of its teaching for debates among 17th century French Calvinists. Indeed, the catechism and its early interpretation provide a precedent for Amyraut's position which pre-dates the Synod of Dordt by some thirty years. Consistent with all that Amyraut found in Calvin, the *Heidelberg Catechism* asserts not only that the church is 'chosen to everlasting life' (Q. 54) but also that 'Christ bore in body and soul the wrath of God against the sin of the whole human race' (Q. 37). Modern attempts[81] to adapt the sense of these statements to a high Calvinist stance are surely invalidated by the views of David Pareus (1548-1622), pupil of Dr Zacharias Ursinus (1534-83), co-author with Caspar Olevianus (1536-87) of the catechism. Reflecting his teacher's theology, Pareus (who actually completed and published Ursinus' own commentary on the catechism in 1585)[82] affirmed that as Christ 'died for all, in respect to the sufficiency of his ransom; and for the faithful alone in respect of the efficacy of the same, so also he willed to die for all in general, as touching the sufficiency of his merit....But he willed to die for the elect alone as touching the efficacy of his death.'[83] Thus it was Ursinus-Pareus, not Beza, who perpetuated a view more arguably 'Calvinist' after the reformer's death. Despite some minor ambiguities, this is the soteriology endorsed at the Synod of Dordt to which Amyraut appealed at the Synod of Alençon. Thus the theology of the *Heidelberg Catechism* constitutes a sold link between Calvin's and Amyraut's.

By careful reading of the following statements of Calvin, the reader will be able to judge the validity of these introductory observations. The quotations - which the present writer claims to be full though not exhaustive - follow a biblical order in view of the preponderance of commentary material. Unlike Daillé's similar scheme in his *Apologia pro duabis...Synodis* (Amsterdam, 1655), quotations from sermons, treatises and other sources are appropriately placed to reinforce the biblical commentary. The evidence suggests that Calvin held a consistent position; there is no 'early' and 'late' Calvin on this subject. What he grasped in the 1530s he constantly proclaimed throughout his ministry. Thus from 1540 - the year in which the Commentary on Romans appeared - to 1564 - the year of his Last Will and death, it will be possible to discover Calvin's precise position on the atonement. The final 1559 edition of the *Institutes* will be seen to harmonize with the author's statements from other sources.

Postscript: For a discussion of Amyraut's *Brief Traitté de la Predestination* (1634) see my *Amyraut Affirmed or 'Owenism, a Caricature of Calvinism'* (2004), - A reply to Ian Hamilton's *Amyraldianism - is it modified Calvinism?* (2003). Here I demonstrate that far from being alien to Calvinism, Amyraldianism - with its 'double-reference, dual-divine intention' view of the atonement - may be seen as an authentic expression of John Calvin's misunderstood teaching. Thus I argue on historical and biblical grounds that the ultra-orthodox theology of John Owen and the *Westminster Confession of Faith* demands a radical reassessment and revision.

Notes to the Introduction

1.   See *Institutes* I. xvii. 2; xviii. 3.
2.   See *La Bible* (Geneva, 1588), 60. The 'world' is defined as 'the chosen among men without distinction of nation or character'. See also B. G. Armstrong, 'Geneva and the theology and politics of French Calvinism: the embarrassment of the 1588 edition of the Bible of the pastors and professors of Geneva' in *Calvinus Ecclesiae Genevensis Custos*, ed. W. H. Neuser (New York, 1983).
3.   See J. Owen, *Death of Death* in *Works*, ed. W. H. Goold (Edinburgh, 1850), x. 344.
4.   Ibid., x. 336.
5.   *Tracts* (Edinburgh, 1849), ii, 527.
6   See B. G. Armstrong, *Calvinism and the Amyraut Heresy: Protestant Scholasticism and Humanism in Seventeenth Century France* (Madison, 1969); A. C. Clifford, *Atonement and Justification: English Evangelical Theology, 1640-1790 - An Evaluation* (Oxford, 1990), 69ff. Also, 'Geneva Revisited or Calvinism Revised' in *Churchman*, 100.4 (1986), 323-334; and 'John Calvin and the Confessio Fidei Gallicana' in *The Evangelical Quarterly*, 58.3 (1986), 195-206. The reader is also referred to Appendix A, 'Did John Calvin teach Limited Atonement?' from Dr C. Daniel's unpublished PhD thesis, 'John Gill and Hypercalvinism' (Edinburgh, 1983), 777-828. After the most meticulous scrutiny, Dr Daniel answers the question with a decided negative! For evidence of Beza's 'ultra orthodox' deviations from Calvin's thought, see R. T. Kendall, *Calvin and English Calvinism to 1649* (Oxford, 1979) 29ff; also Michael Jinkins, 'Theodore Beza: Continuity and Regression in the Reformed Tradition', EQ 64.2 (1992), 131-154.
7.   See John Quick, *Synodicon in Gallia Reformata* (London, 1692), ii. 352-7; 455; 554-61.
8.   See B. G. Armstrong, *Calvinism and the Amyraut Heresy*, 158-69.
The second Dordt Canon states that the 'death of the Son of God is the only and most perfect sacrifice and satisfaction for sins, of infinite value and worth, abundantly sufficient to expiate the sins of the whole world....That, however, many who have been called by the gospel neither repent nor believe in Christ but perish in unbelief does not happen because of any defect or insufficiency in the sacrifice of Christ offered on the cross, but through their own fault....For this was the most free counsel of God the father, that the life-giving and saving efficacy of the most precious death of His Son should extend to all the elect' (Arts. 3, 6, 7). See *The Creeds of the Evangelical Protestant Churches*, ed. H. B. Smith and P. Schaff (London, 1877), 586f.

At the National Synod of Alençon (1637), Amyraut (and Testard) declared that 'Jesus Christ died for all men sufficiently, but for the elect only effectually: and that consequentially his intention was to die for all men in respect of the sufficiency of his satisfaction, but for the elect only in respect of its quickening and saving virtue and efficacy; which is to say, that Christ's will was that the sacrifice of his cross should be of an infinite price and value, and most abundantly sufficient to expiate the sins of the whole world; yet nevertheless the efficacy of his death appertains only unto the elect;...for this was the most free counsel and gracious purpose both of God the Father, in giving his Son for the salvation of mankind, and of the Lord Jesus Christ, in suffering the pains of death, that the efficacy thereof should particularly belong unto all the elect, and to them only...' (Quick, *Synodicon*, ii. 354).

Consistent with Dordt's teaching on election and predestination (First Canon, Art. 7), Amyraut declared that 'there is none other decree of predestination of men unto eternal life and salvation, than the unchangeable purpose of God, by which according to the most free and good pleasure of his will, he hath out of mere grace chosen in Jesus Christ unto salvation before the foundation of the world, a certain number of men in themselves neither better nor more worthy than others, and that he hath decreed to give them unto Jesus Christ to be saved...' (Ibid., 355).

9.   Daillé clearly states that 'The election of God is the choice which he makes, according to his good pleasure, of certain persons, to call them to the knowledge of himself, and to the glory of his salvation. And this term, election, signifies sometimes the resolution he has taken in his eternal counsel to choose and call them, which the Scripture elsewhere calls the determinate purpose of God, Eph. 1: 11' (*An Exposition of Colossians* (1648), ed. J. Sherman, (Edinburgh, 1863), 201). With equal Amyraldian clarity, Daillé expounds the atonement: 'For though 'he is the propitiation for the sins of the whole world,' 1 John 2: 2, and the worth of his sacrifice so great that it abundantly suffices to expiate all the crimes of the universe; and although the salvation obtained by him is really offered, and by his will, unto all men; yet none actually enjoy it but those that enter into his communion by faith, and are by that means in him, as that clause of his covenant expressly imports, 'God so loved the world that he gave his only begotten Son, that whosoever believeth in him should not perish, but have everlasting life,' John 3: 16' (Ibid., 27).

10.   *The Controversy over the Theology of Saumur, 1635-1650: Disrupting debates among the Huguenots in complicated circumstances,* (Amsterdam & Maarssen, 1988), 405, 439. This work should be read as a historical companion piece to Armstrong's book. It provides biographical information of the various theologians involved.

11.   The fact that Paul commences with predestination in Ephesians does not challenge this observation. Being a 'church epistle', it was fitting for the Apostle to provide direct teaching for 'internal consumption'. Even here, there is no trace of 'limited atonement' teaching. Regarding Eph. 5: 25, see my *Atonement and Justification*, 145. However, the Roman church received instruction appropriate to their unique evangelistic opportunities at the heart of the Roman Empire.

12.   Thus Amyraut declared: 'And whereas they have made distinct decrees in this counsel of God, the first of which is to save all men through Jesus Christ, if they shall believe in him; the second to give faith unto some particular persons: they declared, that they did this upon none other account, than of accomodating it unto that manner and order which the spirit of man observeth in his reasonings for the succour of his own infirmity; they otherwise believing, that though they considered this decree as diverse, yet it was formed in God in one and the self same moment, without any succession of thought, or order of priority and posteriority. The will of this most supreme and incomprehensible Lord, being but one only eternal act in him; so that could we but conceive of things as they be in him from all eternity, we should comprehend these decrees of God by one only act of our understanding, as in truth they be but one only act of his eternal and unchangeable will' (Quick, *Synodicon*, ii. 355). This statement, together with Amyraut's theological kinship with Calvin (see #27, 73, 83), surely answers Stephen Strehle's observations in 'Universal Grace and Amyraldianism' in *The Westminster Theological Journal*, 51. 2 (1989), 354ff. Thus the present author corrects his erroneous comment on Amyraut in *Atonement and Justification*, 154. There is no difference between Baxter and Amyraut on the order of the decrees.

13.   Van Stam, op. cit., 431.

14.   See G. Smeaton, *The Doctrine of the Holy Spirit* (Edinburgh, 1889; facs., London, 1958), 322ff.

15.   See R. Nicole: review of Van Stam, *WTJ* 54.2 (1992), 396.

16.   See M. Prestwich, 'The Huguenots under Richelieu and Mazarin, 1629-61: A Golden Age?' in *Huguenots in Britain and their French Background 1550-1800*, ed, I. Scouloudi (London, 1987), 186.

17.   See P. Joutard, 'The Revocation of the Edict of Nantes: End or Renewal of French

Protestantism?' in *International Calvinism 1541-1715*, ed. M. Prestwich (Oxford, 1985), 343.

18.   See M. Prestwich, 'The Huguenots under Richelieu and Mazarin', 194.

19.   See Nicole, op. cit., 396.

20.   *The Triumph of Faith* (London, 1698), 24. For further evidence see article on Amyraut in P. Bayle, *Dictionary Historical and Critical*, 2nd ed. (London,1734), i. 260-66.

21.   See J. Daillé, *Apologie des Eglises Réformées* (Paris, 1633); (Eng. tr.): *An Apologie for the Reformed Churches* (Cambridge, 1653).

22.   See J. Claude, *La Defense de la Reformation* (Quevilly, 1673); (Eng. tr.): *A Defence of the Reformation* (London, 1683). Together with Daillé jnr and others, Claude opposed the *Formula Concensus Helvetica* (1675). Framed by Francis Turretin of Geneva (1623-87) and others, this anti-Amyraldian document had no authority outside Switzerland. Within fifty years it was abrogated, partly through the zealous efforts of Turretin's son, Alphonso! (See G. P. Fisher, *History of Christian Doctrine* (Edinburgh, 1896), 345).

23.   *France...Forgotten Mission Field* (Welwyn, 1971), 93.

24.   *See Traitté de la composition d'un sermon* in *Les oeuvres postumes de Mr Claude*, i, (Amsterdam, 1688); (Eng. tr.): *Essay on the Composition of a Sermon*, ed. C. Simeon, (Cambridge, 1796).

25.   Orna-Ornstein, op. cit., 94. The author blames the views of Claude Pajon (1626-85) on Amyraldian 'tendencies' (ibid., 93) but J. Claude opposed Pajonism (see Fisher, op. cit., 346).

26.   Having urged preachers to consider 'the happy success of the Gospel in the conversion of men' resulting from its 'victorious and triumphant power' (*Essay*, ed. Simeon, 31), Claude eloquently warns against presuming on the certainty of a death-bed conversion: 'I own farther, that a true and sincere conversion at the last hour of life is not altogether unexampled: God shows us now and then one, to make us admire the marvels of his grace and the *depths of his electing love*. But, granting all this, I beg you also to remark the following truths. First, true and sincere conversions in the last moments of life are so rare, that God has left us but one example in all Scripture; and even that example is singular in its circumstances; it is that of the converted thief. But, besides that nothing less than a cross, that is, a most infamous and cruel death, was necessary to affect him, there was needed also, to work this great miracle, the dying presence of the eternal Son of God. It was in that grand action, *in which our Redeemer offered his eternal sacrifice for the whole world;* in that action, in which he caused the smoke of his oblation to ascend, as it were, from earth to heaven, in a sweet-smelling savour to God the Father; in that action in which the sun was eclipsed, the earth trembled, the graves opened, the veil of the temple was rent in twain; it was, I say, very just that the Saviour's blood should work such a miracle, and that the Spirit of grace, to honour the death of the eternal Son of God, should display his power in an extraordinary manner. But let no one imagine, from this example, that it shall be so with him. Jesus Christ does not die every day, his blood was shed but once; and who told you, that what he did in the act of his sacrifice, he will repeat again every day?' (Ibid., 90, emphases mine).

27.   Orna-Ornstein, op. cit., 93.

28.   J-M. Berthoud, 'John Calvin and the Spread of the Gospel in France' in Fulfilling the Great Commission (*Westminster Conference Papers*, 1992), 30.

29.   Quick, *Synodicon*, ii. 354.

30.   Berthoud, 'John Calvin', 37.

31.   See Armstrong, op. cit., 38ff and 127ff.

32.   See J-M. Berthoud, *Des Acts de l'Eglise: Le Christianisme en Suisse Romande* (Lausanne, 1993), 59-79. See my account of Brousson's ministry and martyrdom 'Reformed Pastoral Theology under the Cross: John Quick and Claude Brousson', *EQ* 66:4 (1994), 291-306.

33.   See Quick, *Synodicon*, ii. 510.

[handwritten marginal notes: "Death bed Conversion", "only once in Scripture"]

34.   C. Brousson, 'Lettre aux Pasteurs de France réfugiés dans les Etats protestants' in *Lettres et Opuscules de feu Monsr. Claude Brousson* (Utrecht, 1701), 22 (cited in Berthoud, *Des Acts de l'Eglise*, 69). I am grateful to Mrs C. Lusk of Milnrow, Rochdale, Lancs. for translating an extract of this letter.

35.   Van Stam, op. cit., 38.

36.   Ibid., 54f.

37.   Ibid., 428f.

38.   J. Owen, *Death of Death* in *Works*, x. 236.

39.   Brousson, 'Lettre aux Pasteurs de France', 23.

40.   Quick is careful to rescue Amyraut from the charge of crypto-Arminianism: 'The orthodox do judge...that the efficacy of Christ's death which consisteth in the communication of the Spirit of grace doth exert itself in none other persons but in the elect only. But as for others, although they may be called with an outward calling, yet because they be not inwardly enlightened, they must of necessity abide in their impenitency. Amyrald (sic) did always believe this doctrine of the orthodox to be true and hath demonstrated the truth of it by invincible arguments in the 14th chapter of his Defense of Mr Calvin' (*Icones Sacrae Gallicanae* [1700], Dr Williams's Library Quick MSS (transcript) 6. 38-39 (35), 1024. Like Calvin, Amyraut attributes all ability for good in man to the grace and providence of God (ibid., 1019). Distinguishing between natural and moral ability, the Amyraldians affirmed that human impotency arises from 'malice of heart' rather than physical or mental incapacity (see Quick, *Synodicon*, ii. 356f). Calvin clearly assumed this (see *Inst.* II. ii. 12f). In short, sinners are 'unwilling' rather than 'unable' to turn to Christ.

41.   H. M. Baird, *The Huguenots and the Revocation of the Edict of Nantes* (London, 1895), ii. 470 (Ostervald's dates added).

42.   R. Heath, *The Reformation in France* (London, 1888), ii. 85.

43.   Berthoud, *Des Actes de l'Eglise*, 96.

44.   See Van Stam, op. cit., 446f. Like Amyraut, Drelincourt had great admiration for Calvin. He replied to malicious Roman Catholic attacks on the reformer's memory in *La Defense de Calvin* (Geneva, 1667). This is the work referred to by John Tillotson (rather than the one indicated by the editors) in a letter to Matthew Sylvester dated 3 February 1691/2 given in N. H. Keeble and G. F. Nuttall, *Calendar of the Correspondence of Richard Baxter* (Oxford, 1991), ii. 330.

45.   See A. C. Clifford, 'John Calvin and the Confessio Fidei Gallicana', *EQ* 58.3 (1986), 195-206.

46.   See Van Stam, op. cit., 442ff.

47.   Berthoud, *Des Actes de l'Eglise*, 83.

48.   Ibid., 95.

49.   E. Hugues, *Antoine Court: Histoire de la Restauration du Protestantisme en France au XVIIIe siécle* (Paris, 1872), i. 32f.

50.   See A. C. Clifford, *Atonement and Justification*, 102ff.

51.   Cited in R. Baxter, *Catholic Theologie* (London, 1675), II. 52. See the *Latin work, Anatome arminianismi* (Lugduni-Batavorum, 1619).

52.   Hugues, *Antoine Court*, 51.

53.   J. F. Ostervald, *The Grounds and Principles of the Christian Religion explained in a Catechetical Discourse for the Instruction of Young People*, tr. H. Wanley, 6th ed. (London, 1751), 49. The author's work was first published in French in Neuchatel (1702). Not having access to the abridgement mentioned by Baird, the unabridged version is used. Besides, this facilitates a more accurate assessment of Ostervald's theology.

Consistent with the author's universal language, John 3: 16 is quoted (at p. 76) in a manner typical of Calvin (see #8, 16, 18, 46, 57) without the least sign of a 'Bezan' gloss. Ostervald is equally comfortable (at p. 71) quoting a classical 'limited atonement' proof text, 'for He shall save his people from their sins' (Matt. 1: 21). As Calvin makes clear (see #24), this verse is no threat to an

'Amyraldian' view of the atonement.

54.   J. Calvin, *Catechism of the Church of Geneva*, in *Tracts* (Edinburgh, 1849), ii. 47. This was first published in Geneva (1545).

55.   C. Drelincourt, *A Catechism, or Familiar Instructions on the Principal Points of the Christian Religion* (London, 1698), 64. This work was first published in Paris (1642).

56.   Calvin, op. cit., 50.

57.   Ibid., 43.

58.   Ibid., 51.

59.   Drelincourt, op. cit., 27f.

60.   Ostervald, op. cit., 197.

61.   Calvin, op. cit., 76.

62.   Drelincourt, op. cit., 70.

63.   Ostervald, op. cit., 200.

64.   Drelincourt, op. cit., 71.

65.   Ostervald, op. cit., 63

66.   See *Inst*. I: xviii: 1.

67.   Calvin, *Catechism*, 41.

68.   Berthoud, *Des Actes de l'Eglise*, 82.

69.   Orna-Ornstein, op. cit., 104.

70.   See A. C. Clifford, *Atonement and Justification*, 26; H. Boersma, *A Hot Pepper Corn: Richard Baxter's Doctrine of Justification in its Seventeenth-Century Context of Controversy* (Zoetermeer, The Netherlands, 1993), 25ff.

71.   E. Hugues (ed), *Mémoires d'Antoine Court* (Paris, 1885), 26.

72.   Baxter wrote: 'God hath blessed it with unexpected success beyond all the rest that I have written, except the 'Saints' Rest'....Yet God would make some further use of it, for Mr Stoop, the pastor of the French church in London, being driven hence by the displeasure of superiors, was pleased to translate it into elegant French, and print it in a very curious letter' (*Reliquiae Baxterianae*, ed. M. Sylvester, (London, 1696), I. 115). For Jean-Baptise Stouppe (d. 1692), see Y. Jaulmes, *The French Protestant Church of London and the Huguenots* (London, 1993), 38.

73.   R. Baxter, *A Call to the Unconverted* in *The Practical Works of Richard Baxter* (Grand Rapids, Mich., 1981), 455.

74.   Berthoud, *Des Actes de l'Eglise,* 95. Similar comments are made about the Northampton academy of Dr Philip Doddridge (1702-51), a 'disciple' of Baxter. Interestingly, Doddridge's and Court's academies both started in 1729. The fact that their successors deviated from the biblical basis of their founders does not invalidate Court's and Doddridge's balanced theological stance. All shades of Protestantism suffered from the blight of the enlightenment. Those who stood aloof from these trends often lapsed in an equally unbiblical hypercalvinism. For Doddridge's 'Baxterian' alias 'Amyraldian' theology, see A. C. Clifford, 'The Christian Mind of Philip Doddridge', *EQ* 56.4 (1984), 227-42. Doddridge was acquainted with the continuing persecution in France. In the last year of his life (1751), he wrote: 'I have read and heard a great deal of the sufferings of our Protestant brethren in France; I have conversed with those who saw their assemblies dissolved, their temples ruined, and their dead torn out of the graves and given to the fowls of the air. I have read the letters of their pastors, and their martyrs; and the incomparable discourses of Superville and Saurin, which so pathetically represent their sufferings...Quick's *Synodicon* I have. The *Icones* (see n. 40) I shall be very glad to see...' (*Correspondence and Diary of Philip Doddridge*, ed. J. D. Humphreys, (London, 1831), v. 187ff).

75.   H. M. Baird, *The Huguenots*, 470f.

76.   Ibid., 471.

77. See A. Cochrane (ed.), *Reformed Confessions of the Sixteenth Century* (London, 1966), 305ff.

78. H. M. Baird, *The Huguenots*, 473.

79. See Ostervald, op. cit., 117ff. Berthoud might take exception to a lack of reference to imputed righteousness in Ostervald's treatment of justification. Yet justification by faith in Christ alone is fully and clearly stated. While good works are insisted upon for salvation as the fruit of a living, justifying faith, any suggestion that they possess merit before God is strongly repudiated. All in all, if high orthodox divines might take exception to Ostervald's position, the evidence suggests that Calvin and many other continental Reformed theologians would have found no reason to dissent from Ostervald. See A. C. Clifford, *Atonement and Justification*, 169ff and Boersma, op. cit., 220ff.

80. For Court and Rabaut, see Heath, op. cit., ii. 85ff and Samuel Smiles, *The Huguenots in France after the Revocation of the Edict of Nantes* (London, 1875), 205ff. Even from a high Calvinist perspective, the theology of Rabaut's early preaching challenges Baird's observations on 18th century French Calvinism. While one specimen does not constitute conclusive proof, a rare 'desert sermon' fragment dating from 1753 (from the appendix to the letters of Paul Rabaut to Antoine Court) suggests a 'limited atonement' view: 'But without doubt, the holy word that I have announced to you will not return unto the Lord without effect. Without doubt among those who listen to me are sinners who labour and are heavy laden, souls hungering and thirsting after the righteousness of Jesus Christ. Oh! go with confidence to this divine Saviour; it is you whom He calls; it is you whose thirst He will quench, whose hunger He will satisfy; it is for you that He shed His blood; it is to you that He offers the treasure of His grace. Go, then, to Him, with a firm assurance that you will find in His blood the remission of your sins, and the principle of a new life...' (Heath, op. cit., ii. 111). If anything, Rabaut sounds more 'ultra' than the high orthodox; at least the latter generally believed that the gospel call was indiscriminate even though - as the Amyraldians also held - its efficacy was limited to the elect. In view of his support for Gibert seventeen years later and his probable acquiescence in the 1771 synod decision to approve Ostervald's catechism, it is likely that Rabaut's early apparent high Calvinism had 'moderated'.

81. See H. Hoeksema, *The Triple Knowledge: An Exposition of the Heidelberg Catechism* (Grand Rapids, Mich., 1976), i. 529-43, 641-2; see also W. R. Godfrey, 'Reformed thought on the extent of the atonement', WTJ 37 (1975), 151f.

82. See W. R. Godfrey, op. cit., 148.

83. Z. Ursinus, *The Commentary on the Heidelberg Catechism*, ed. G. W. Williard (Phillipsburg, NJ, 1985), 223. While the medieval theologians Peter Lombard and Thomas Aquinas resorted to the sufficiency-efficiency distinction, David Pareus also employed it as part of a measured exegetical response to the biblical data: 'In answering this question [did Christ die for all?] we must make a distinction, so as to harmonise those passages of Scriptures which seem to teach contradictory doctrines. In some places Christ is said to have died for all, and for the whole world (1 Jn. 2: 2, Heb. 2: 9, 2 Cor. 5: 15, 1 Tim. 2: 6). The Scriptures, on the contrary, affirm in many places, that Christ died, prayed, offered himself, etc, only for many, for the elect, for his own people, for the church, for his sheep, etc (Jn. 17: 9, Matt. 20: 28; 1: 21, Heb. 9: 28, Isa. 53:11, Eph. 5: 25). What shall we say in view of these seemingly opposite passages of Scripture? Does the word of God contradict itself? By no means. But this will be the case, unless these declarations, which in some places seem to teach that Christ died for all, and others that he died for a part only, can be reconciled by a proper and satisfactory distinction, which distinction, or reconciliation, is two-fold' (ibid., 221-2). For Calvin's use of the distinction, see #19, 42, 84, 85.

The Sources

Old Testament comments are taken from the Calvin Translation Society (CTS) Commentaries (Edinburgh, 1845-). New Testament comments are taken from the Oliver & Boyd/St Andrew Press edition (Edinburgh, 1959-72). For the *Institutes of the Christian Religion*, reference may be made to either the Beveridge (CTS, 1845) or Battles (Westminster Press/SCM, Philadelphia/London 1960) editions. Page references are only given for sermon and treatise quotations. The quotations from *Sermons on Job, Deuteronomy, Galatians and Timothy & Titus* come from the Arthur Golding translations (London, 1574-83). With the exception of Galatians, these are available in Banner of Truth facsimile. The new Banner of Truth edition of *Sermons on 2 Samuel*, tr. Douglas Kelly (Edinburgh, 1992) is also quoted. The Isaiah sermon extracts are taken from the James Clarke edition, tr. T. H. L. Parker (London, 1956). Extracts of the *Sermons on Christ's Passion* are from the Baker edition, tr. L. Nixon (Grand Rapids, 1950). For the *Sermons on Ephesians*, the modern Banner of Truth edition (Edinburgh, 1973) is used. For Calvin's *Treatise on Predestination*, see the James Clarke edition, tr. J. K. S. Reid (London, 1961). Quotations from the *Antidote to the Council of Trent*, the Genevan Catechism and *Forms of Prayers for the Church* are taken from the CTS edition of the *Tracts*. The extract from Calvin's Last Will comes from *The Letters of John Calvin* (Banner of Truth edition, Edinburgh, 1980).

Note: Calvin's *Sermons on Galatians* were published in a modern edition by The Banner of Truth Trust in1997.

John Calvin
(1509-64)

Extracts from John Calvin's Writings

1. Now Paul assumes it as an axiom which is received among all the pious....that the whole human race is obnoxious to a curse, and therefore that the holy people are blessed only through the grace of the Mediator...I therefore thus interpret the present place; that God promises to his servant Abram that blessing which shall afterwards flow down to all people.

Comment on Genesis 12: 3

2. Christ was vividly represented in the person of the high priest...[who] bore the people itself upon his shoulders and before his breast, in such a manner that in the person of one, all might be presented familiarly before God.

Comment on Exodus 39: 1

3. We have stated elsewhere why the priests were to be dressed in garments different from others, since he who is the mediator between God and men should be free from all impurity and stain...Thus then the holy fathers were reminded, that under the image of a mortal man, another Mediator was promised, who, for the reconciliation of the human race, should present Himself before God with perfect and more than angelic *purity*.

Comment on Leviticus 16: 3

4. Christ...the Lamb of God, whose offering blotted out the sins of the world...

Comment on Leviticus 16: 7

5. God could bear no defect in the priests; it follows, then, that a man of angelic purity was to be expected, who should reconcile God to the world.

Comment on Leviticus 21: 17

6. ...the salvation brought by Christ is common to the whole human race, inasmuch as Christ, the author of salvation, is descended from Adam, the common father of us all.

Institutes, II. xiii. 3

7. First, we must understand that as long as Christ remains outside of us, and we are separated from him, all that he has suffered and done for the salvation of the human race remains useless and of no value for us.

Institutes, III. i. 1

8. It is true that Saint John saith generally, that [God] loved the world. And why? For Jesus Christ offereth himself generally to all men without exception to be their redeemer...Thus we see three degrees of the love that God hath shewed us in our Lord Jesus Christ. The first is in respect of the redemption that was purchased in the person of him that gave himself to death for us, and became accursed to reconcile us to God his Father. That is the first degree of love, which extendeth to all men, inasmuch as Jesus Christ reacheth out his arms to call and allure all men both great and small, and to win them to him. But there is a special love for those to whom the gospel is preached: which is that God testifieth unto them that he will make them partakers of the benefit that was purchased for them by the death and passion of his Son. And forasmuch as we be of that number, therefore we are double bound already to our God: here are two bonds which hold us as it were strait tied unto him. Now let us come to the third bond, which dependeth upon the third love that God sheweth us: which is that he not only causeth the gospel to be preached unto us, but also maketh us

to feel the power thereof, so as we know him to be our Father and Saviour, not doubting but that our sins are forgiven us for our Lord Jesus Christ's sake, who bringeth us the gift of the Holy Ghost, to reform us after his own image.

Sermons on Deuteronomy, 167

9.   ...our Lord Jesus Christ, who is the life and salvation of the world,...

Sermons on 2 Samuel, 66

10.   For instance, let me think of myself in this way:...that God has bestowed grace upon the human race (in general) but that he has shown his grace to me (in particular), with the result that I am especially obligated to him.

Sermons on 2 Samuel, 357

11.   So, as it says in the Psalm [Ps. 51?], our Lord Jesus Christ has paid the debts of all sinners. That is what I have mentioned from Isaiah: that all the chastisements were laid upon him (Isa. 53:4). What is this chastisement, if not satisfaction for all the sins that we have committed?

Sermons on 2 Samuel, 576

12.   True it is that the effect of [Christ's] death comes not to the whole world. Nevertheless, forasmuch as it is not in us to discern between the righteous and the sinners that go to destruction, but that Jesus Christ has suffered his death and passion as well for them as for us, therefore it behoves us to labour to bring every man to salvation, that the grace of our Lord Jesus Christ may be available to them.

Sermons on Job, 548 (later interpolation deleted)

13.   Let us fall down before the face of our good God...that it may please Him to grant His grace, not only to us, but also to all people and nations of the earth, bringing back all poor ignorant souls from the miserable bondage of error and darkness, to the right way of salvation...

Sermons on Job, 751 (Calvin's usual end of sermon prayer)

14.   The sinner, if he would find mercy, must look to the sacrifice of Christ, which expiated the sins of the world, glancing, at the same time, for the confirmation of his faith, to Baptism and the Lord's Supper; for it were vain to imagine that God, the Judge of the world, would receive us again into his favour in any other way than through a satisfaction made to his justice.

Comment on Psalm 51: 9

15.   Diligent as [David] was, therefore, in the practice of sacrifice, resting his whole dependence upon the satisfaction of Christ, who atoned for the sins of the world, he could yet honestly declare that he brought nothing to God in the shape of compensation, and that he trusted entirely to a gratuitous reconciliation.

Comment on Psalm 51: 16

16.   Hitherto he addressed the Jews alone, as if to them alone salvation belonged, but now he extends his discourse farther. He invites the whole world to the hope of salvation, and at the same time brings a charge of ingratitude against all the nations, who, being devoted to their own errors, purposely avoided, as it were, the light of life; for what could be more base than to reject deliberately their own salvation?...the Lord...invites all without exception to come to him...Now, we must 'look to him' with the eye of faith, so as to embrace the salvation which is exhibited to all through Christ; for 'God so loved the world that he gave his only begotten Son, that whosoever believeth in him may not perish.' (John 3:16).

Comment on Isaiah 45: 22

17.   Yet I approve of the ordinary reading, that he alone bore the punishment of many, because on him was laid the guilt of the whole world. It is evident from other passages, and especially from the fifth chapter of the Epistle to the Romans, that 'many' sometimes denotes 'all'.

Comment on Isaiah 53: 12

18.   Yet I approve of the common reading, that He alone bore the punishment of many, because the guilt of the whole world was laid upon Him. It is evident from other passages...that 'many' sometimes denotes 'all'...That, then, is how our Lord Jesus bore the sins and iniquities of many. But in fact, this word 'many' is often as good as equivalent to 'all'. And indeed, our Lord Jesus was offered to all the world. For it is not speaking of three or four when it says: 'God so loved the world, that He spared not His only Son.' But yet we must notice what the Evangelist adds in this passage: 'That whosoever believes in Him shall not perish but obtain eternal life.' Our Lord Jesus suffered for all and there is neither great nor small who is not inexcusable today, for we can obtain salvation in Him. Unbelievers who turn away from Him and who deprive themselves of Him by their malice are today doubly culpable. For how will they excuse their ingratitude in not receiving the blessing in which they could share by faith? And let us realize that if we come flocking to our Lord Jesus Christ, we shall not hinder one another and prevent Him being sufficient for each of us...Let us not fear to come to Him in great numbers, and each one of us bring his neighbours, seeing that He is sufficient to save us all.

Sermons on Isaiah 53, 136, 141-4

19.   ...Not only were the death and passion of our Lord Jesus Christ sufficient for the salvation of the world, but that God will make them efficacious and that we shall see the fruit of them and even feel and experience it.

Sermons on Isaiah 53, 116

20.   For God, who is perfect righteousness, cannot love the iniquity which he sees in all. All of us, therefore, have that within which deserves the hatred of God...Our acquittal is in this - that the guilt which made us liable to punishment was transferred to the head of the Son of God [Isa. 53:12]...For, were not Christ a victim, we could have no sure conviction of his being...our substitute-ransom and propitiation.

Institutes II. xvi. 3, 5, 6

21.   Now we must see how God wishes all to be converted...But we must remark that God puts on a twofold character: for he here wishes to be taken at his word. As I have already said, the Prophet does not here dispute with subtlety about his incomprehensible plans, but wishes to keep our attention close to God's word. Now what are the contents of this word? The law, the prophets, and the gospel. Now all are called to repentance, and the hope of salvation is promised them when they repent: this is true, since God rejects no returning sinner: he pardons all without exception; meanwhile, this will of God which he sets forth in his word does not prevent him from decreeing before the world was created what he would do with every individual...

Comment on Ezekiel 18: 23

22.   I contend that, as the prophet [Ezekiel] is exhorting to penitence, it is no wonder that he pronounces God willing that all be saved. But the mutual relation between threats and promises shows such forms of speech to be conditional...So again...the promises which invite all men to salvation...do not simply and positively declare what God has decreed in His secret counsel but what he is prepared to do for all who are brought to faith and repentance...Now this is not contradictory of His secret counsel, by which he determined to convert none but His elect. He cannot rightly on this account be thought variable, because as lawgiver He illuminates all with the

external doctrine of life. But in the other sense, he brings to life whom He will, as Father regenerating by the Spirit only His sons.

Concerning the Eternal Predestination of God, 105-6

23.   ...God had chosen the family of Abraham, that the world's redeemer might be born of it...although we know that from the time that God made a covenant with Abraham, the Redeemer was particularly promised to his seed, we also know that from the very fall of man He was needed by all, as indeed He was from that time destined for all the world...It would have done us no good for Christ to have been given by the Father as the author of salvation, if He had not been available to all without distinction...We should know that salvation is openly displayed to all the human race, for in all reality He is called son of Noah and son of Adam...

Comment on Matthew 1: 1-17; Luke 3: 23-38

24.   He says, For...he...shall save his people from their sins...We must determine that the whole human race was appointed to destruction, since its salvation depends on Christ...Doubtless, by Christ's people the angel intends the Jews, over whom He was set as Head and King, but as soon after the nations were to be ingrafted into the race of Abraham, this promise of salvation is extended openly to all who gather by faith into the one body of the Church.

Comment on Matthew 1: 21

25.   When the Father calls Him the Beloved...He declares that He is the Mediator in whom He reconciles the world to Himself.

Comment on Matthew 17: 5

26.   From this it follows that our reconciliation with God is free, for the only price paid for it is Christ's death...'Many' is used, not for a definite number, but for a large number, in that He sets Himself over against all others. And this is the meaning also in Rom. 5:15, where Paul is not talking of a part of mankind but of the whole human race.

Comment on Matthew 20: 28

27.   Seeing that in His Word He calls all alike to salvation, and this is the object of preaching, that all should take refuge in His faith and protection, it is right to say that He wishes all to gather to Him. Now the nature of the Word shows us that here there is no description of the secret counsel of God - just His wishes. Certainly those whom He wishes effectively to gather, He draws inwardly by His Spirit, and calls them not merely by man's outward voice. If anyone objects that it is absurd to split God's will, I answer that this is exactly our belief, that His will is one and undivided: but because our minds cannot plumb the profound depths of His secret election to suit our infirmity, the will of God is set before us as double.

Comment on Matthew 23: 37

28.   ...The Son of God went to face death of His own will, to reconcile the world to the Father...the spontaneous sacrifice by which all the world's transgressions were blotted out...

Comment on Matthew 26: 1-2

29.   [Christ's] grave would be of sweet savour to breathe life and salvation upon all the world.

Comment on Matthew 26: 12

30.   Christ offered Himself as a Victim for the salvation of the human race.

Comment on Matthew 26: 1

31.   ...The sacrifice [of Christ] was ordained by the eternal decree of God, to expiate the sins of the world.

Comment on Matthew 26: 24

32.   [Christ was] burdened with the sins of the whole world...

Comment on Matthew 26: 39

33.   Christ...won acquittal for the whole human race.

Comment on Matthew 27: 12

34.   God had ordained [Christ] to be the...(sacrificial outcast) for the expiation of the world's sins.

Comment on Matthew 27: 15

35.   The word many does not mean a part of the world only, but the whole human race: he contrasts many with one, as if to say that he would not be Redeemer of one man, but would meet death to deliver many from their accursed guilt...So when we come to the holy table not only should the general idea come to our mind that the world is redeemed by the blood of Christ, but also each should reckon to himself that his own sins are covered.

Comment on Mark 14: 24

36.   Happy Mary, to have embraced in her heart the promise of God, to have conceived and brought into the world for herself and for all - salvation...God offers His benefits to all without distinction, but faith opens our arms to draw them to our bosom: lack of faith lets them fall, before they reach us.

Comment on Luke 1: 45

37.   Though the angel only addresses the shepherds, he means that the message of salvation which he brings them extends farther, not for their ears alone, but for others also to hear. Understand that the joy was open to all the people, for it was offered to all without distinction. For He is not the God of this one or of that, but He had promised Christ to the whole family of Abraham. That, in great measure, the Jews have lost the joy that was theirs to hold, resulted from their failure to believe. Today also, God invites all men alike to salvation through the Gospel, but the world's ingratitude makes only a few enjoy the grace, which is set out equally for all. While the joy, then, has been confined to a small number, in respect of God, it is called universal. And though the angel is speaking only of the chosen people, yet now with the partition wall gone the same tidings are presented to the whole human race.

Comment on Luke 2: 10

38.   Since Christ desired nothing more than to do the work appointed Him by the Father and knew that the purpose of His calling was to gather the lost sheep of the house of Israel, He wishedHis coming to be the salvation of all. This was why He was moved by compassion and wept overthe approaching destruction of Jerusalem. For when He considered that it had been divinely chosen as the sacred abode, in which should dwell the covenant of eternal salvation, the sanctuary from which salvation should come forth for all the world, He could not help grieving bitterly over its destruction.

Comment on Luke 19: 41

39.   First, whence could that confidence in pardon have sprung, if [the thief] did not sense in Christ's death...a sacrifice of sweet odour, able to expiate the sins of the world?

Comment on Luke 23: 42

40.   [Christ] must be Redeemer of the world...He was there, as it were, in the place of all cursed ones and of all transgressors, and of those who had deserved eternal death.

Sermons on Christ's Passion, 95

41.   [God] willed that [Christ] be the sacrifice to wipe out the sins of the world...

Sermons on Christ's Passion, 123

42.   ...Our Lord made effective for [the pardoned thief on the cross] His death and passion which He suffered and endured for all mankind...

Sermons on Christ's Passion, 151

43.   The Lord Jesus [was] found before the judgement-seat of God in the name of all poor sinners (for He was there, as it were, having to sustain all our burdens)...The death and passion of our Lord Jesus...served...to wipe away the iniquities of the world...

Sermons on Christ's Passion, 155-6

44.   And when he says the sin of the world he extends this kindness indiscriminately to the whole human race, that the Jews might not think the Redeemer has been sent to them alone...John, therefore, by speaking of the sin of the world in general, wanted to make us feel our own misery and exhort us to seek the remedy. Now it is for us to embrace the blessing offered to all, that each may make up his mind that there is nothing to hinder him from finding reconciliation in Christ if only, led by faith, he comes to Him.

Comment on John 1: 29

45.   Christ...was offered as our Saviour...Christ brought life because the heavenly Father does not wish the human race that He loves to perish...But we should remember...that the secret love in which our heavenly Father embraced us to Himself is, since it flows from His eternal good pleasure, precedent to all other causes; but the grace which He wants to be testified to us and by which we are stirred to the hope of salvation, begins with the reconciliation provided through Christ...Thus before we can have any feeling of His Fatherly kindness, the blood of Christ must intercede to reconcile God to us...And He has used a general term [whosoever], both to invite indiscriminately all to share in life and to cut off every excuse from unbelievers. Such is also the significance of the term 'world' which He had used before. For although there is nothing in the world deserving of God's favour, He nevertheless shows He is favourable to the whole world when He calls all without exception to the faith of Christ, which is indeed an entry into life.

Moreover, let us remember that although life is promised generally to all who believe in Christ, faith is not common to all. Christ is open to all and displayed to all, but God opens the eyes only of the elect that they may seek Him by faith...And whenever our sins press hard on us, whenever Satan would drive us to despair, we must hold up this shield, that God does not want us to be overwhelmed in everlasting destruction, for He has ordained His Son to be the Saviour of the world.

Comment on John 3: 16

46.   As also it is said in John 3:16 that God so loved the world that He spared not His own Son, but delivered Him to death for our sakes.

Sermons on Christ's Passion, 48

47.   Again, when they proclaim that Jesus is the Saviour of the world and the Christ, they have undoubtedly learned this from hearing Him...And He declared that the salvation He had brought was common to the whole world, so that they should understand more easily that it belonged to them also.

Comment on John 4: 42

48.   It is no small consolation to godly teachers that, although the larger part of the world does not listen to Christ, He has His sheep whom He knows and by whom He is also known. They must do their utmost to bring the whole world into Christ's fold, but when they do not succeed as they would wish, they must be satisfied with the single thought that those who are sheep will be collected together by their work.

Comment on John 10: 27

49.   Christ...offers salvation to all indiscriminately and stretches out His arms to embrace all, that all may be the more encouraged to repent. And yet He heightens by an important detail the crime of rejecting an invitation so kind and gracious; for it is as if He had said: 'See, I have come to call all; and forgetting the role of judge, my one aim is to attract and rescue from destruction those who already seem doubly ruined.' Hence no man is condemned for despising the Gospel save he who spurns the lovely news of salvation and deliberately decides to bring destruction on himself.

Comment on John 12: 47

50.   For [by Christ's death] we know that by the expiation of sins the world has been reconciled to God...

Comment on John 17: 1

51.   He openly declares that He does not pray for the world, for He is solicitous only for His own flock [the disciples] which He received from the Father's hand. But this might seem absurd; for no better rule of prayer can be found than to follow Christ as our Guide and Teacher. But we are commanded to pray for all, and Christ Himself afterwards prayed for all indiscriminately, 'Father, forgive them; for they know not what they do.' I reply, the prayers which we utter for all are still limited to God's elect. We ought to pray that this and that and every man may be saved and so embrace the whole human race, because we cannot yet distinguish the elect from the reprobate...we pray for the salvation of all whom we know to have been created in God's image and who have the same nature as ourselves; and we leave to God's judgement those whom He knows to be reprobate.

Comment on John 17: 9

52.   ...Moreover, we offer up our prayers unto Thee, O most Gracious God and most merciful Father, for all men in general, that as Thou art pleased to be acknowledged the Saviour of the whole human race by the redemption accomplished by Jesus Christ Thy Son, so those who are still strangers to the knowledge of him, and immersed in darkness, and held captive by ignorance and error, may, by Thy Holy Spirit shining upon them, and by Thy gospel sounding in their ears, be brought back to the right way of salvation, which consists in knowing Thee the true God and Jesus Christ whom Thou hast sent...

Forms of Prayer for the Church
Tracts, ii. 102

53.   The draught appointed to Christ was to suffer the death of the cross for the reconciliation of the world.

Comment on John 18: 11

54.   And surely there is nothing that ought to be more effective in spurring on pastors to devote themselves more eagerly to their duty than if they reflect that it is to themselves that the price of the blood of Christ has been entrusted. For it follows from this, that unless they are faithful in putting out their labour on the Church, not only are they made accountable for lost souls, but they are guilty of sacrilege, because they have profaned the sacred blood of the Son of God, and have made useless the redemption acquired by Him, as far as they are concerned. But it is a hideous and monstrous

crime if, by our idleness, not only the death of Christ becomes worthless, but also the fruit of it is destroyed and perishes...

Comment on Acts 20: 28

55.   For we ought to have a zeal to have the Church of God enlarged, and increase rather than diminish. We ought to have a care also of our brethren, and to be sorry to see them perish: for it is no small matter to have the souls perish which were bought by the blood of Christ.

Sermons on Timothy & Titus, 817

56.   Because God does not work effectually in all men, but only when the Spirit shines in our hearts as the inward teacher, he adds to every one that believeth. The Gospel is indeed offered to all for their salvation, but its power is not universally manifest...When, therefore, the Gospel invites all to partake of salvation without any difference, it is rightly termed the doctrine of salvation. For Christ is there offered, whose proper office is to save that which had been lost, and those who refuse to be saved by Him shall find Him their Judge.

Comment on Romans 1: 16

57.   Faith is the beginning of godliness, from which all those for whom Christ died were estranged...[God] loved us of His own good pleasure, as John tells us (John 3: 16)...We have been reconciled to God by the death of Christ, Paul holds, because His was an expiatory sacrifice by which the world was reconciled to God...

Comment on Romans 5: 6-10

58.   Paul makes grace common to all men, not because it in fact extends to all, but because it is offered to all. Although Christ suffered for the sins of the world, and is offered by the goodness of God without distinction to all men, yet not all receive him.

Comment on Romans 5: 18

59.   ...the price of the blood of Christ is wasted when a weak conscience is wounded, for the most contemptible brother has been redeemed by the blood of Christ. It is intolerable, therefore, that he should be destroyed for the gratification of the belly.

Comment on Romans 14: 15

60.   For one can imagine nothing more despicable than this, that while Christ did not hesitate to die so that the weak might not perish, we, on the other hand, do not care a straw for the salvation of the men and women who have been redeemed at such a price. This is a memorable saying, from which we learn how precious the salvation of our brothers ought to be to us, and not only that of all, but of each individual, in view of the fact that the blood of Christ was poured out for each one...If the soul of every weak person costs the price of the blood of Christ, anyone, who, for the sake of a little bit of meat, is responsible for the rapid return to death of a brother redeemed by Christ, shows just how little the blood of Christ means to him. Contempt like that is therefore an open insult to Christ.

Comment on 1 Corinthians 8: 11

61.   ...God was in Christ and then that by this intervention He was reconciling the world to Himself...Although Christ's coming had its source in the overflowing love of God for us, yet, until men know that God has been propitiated by a mediator, there cannot but be on their side a separation which prevents them from having access to God...[Paul] says again that a commission to offer this reconciliation to us has been given to ministers of the Gospel...He says that as He once suffered, so now every day He offers the fruit of His sufferings to us through the Gospel which He has given to the world as a sure and certain record of His completed work of reconciliation. Thus the duty of

ministers is to apply to us the fruit of Christ's death.

Comment on 2 Corinthians 5: 19

62.   ...when Christ appeared, salvation was sent to the whole world...

Comment on 2 Corinthians 6: 2

63.   Pighius speaks...that Christ, the Redeemer of the whole world, commands the Gospel to be preached promiscuously to all does not seem congruent with special election. But the Gospel is an embassy of peace by which the world is reconciled to God, as Paul teaches (2 Cor. 5:18); and on the same authority it is announced that those who hear are saved. I answer briefly that Christ was so ordained for the salvation of the whole world that He might save those who are given to Him by the Father, that He might be their life whose head He is, and that He might receive those into participation of His benefits whom God by His gratuitous good pleasure adopted as heirs for Himself. Which of these things can be denied?...Even those opposed to me will concede that the universality of the grace of Christ is not better judged than from the preaching of the Gospel. But the solution of the difficulty lies in seeing how the doctrine of the Gospel offers salvation to all. That it is salvific for all I do not deny. But the question is whether the Lord in His counsel here destines salvation equally for all. All are equally called to penitence and faith; the same mediator is set forth for all to reconcile them to the Father - so much is evident. But it is equally evident that nothing can be perceived except by faith, that Paul's word should be fulfilled: the Gospel is the power of God for salvation to all that believe (Rom. 1:16). But what can it be for others but a savour of death to death? as he elsewhere says (2 Cor. 2:16).

Further, since it is clear that out of the many whom God calls by His external voice very few believe, if I prove that the greater part remain unbelieving because God honours with illumination none but those whom He will, then I draw another conclusion. The mercy of God is offered equally to both kinds of men, so that those who are not inwardly taught are rendered only inexcusable....

Concerning the Eternal Predestination of God, 102-3

64.   It is not enough to regard Christ as having died for the salvation of the world; each man must claim the effect and possession of this grace for himself personally.

Comment on Galatians 2: 20

65.   God commends to us the salvation of all men without exception, even as Christ suffered for the sins of the whole world.

Comment on Galatians 5: 12

66.   And he contenteth not himself to say, that Christ gave himself for the world in common, for that had been but a slender saying: but (sheweth that) every of us must apply to himself particularly, the virtue of the death and passion of our Lord Jesus Christ. Whereas it is said that the Son of God was crucified, we must not only think that the same was done for the redemption of the world: but also every of us must on his own behalf join himself to our Lord Jesus Christ, and conclude, It is for me that he hath suffered...But when we once know that the thing was done for the redemption of the whole world, pertaineth to every of us severally: it behoveth every of us to say also on his own behalf, The Son of God hath loved me so dearly, that he hath given himself to death for me...we be very wretches if we accept not such a benefit when it is offered to us...Lo here a warrant for our salvation, so as we ought to think ourselves thoroughly assured of it.

Sermons on Galatians, 106-7

67.   Christ is in a general view the Redeemer of the world, yet his death and passion are of no advantage to any but such as receive that which St Paul shows here. And so we see that when we

once know the benefits brought to us by Christ, and which he daily offers us by his gospel, we must also be joined to him by faith.

Sermons on Ephesians, 55

68.   Also we ought to have good care of those that have been redeemed with the blood of our Lord Jesus Christ. If we see souls which have been so precious to God go to perdition, and we make nothing of it, that is to despise the blood of our Lord Jesus Christ.

Sermons on Ephesians, 521

69.   For the wretched unbelievers and the ignorant have great need to be pleaded for with God; behold them on the way to perdition. If we saw a beast at the point of perishing, we would have pity on it. And what shall we do when we see souls in peril, which are so precious before God, as he has shown in that he has ransomed them with the blood of his own Son. If we see then a poor soul going thus to perdition, ought we not to be moved with compassion and kindness, and should we not desire God to apply the remedy? So then, St. Paul's meaning in this passage is not that we should let the wretched unbelievers alone without having any care for them. We should pray generally for all men...

Sermons on Ephesians, 684-5

70.   He says that this redemption was procured by the blood of Christ, for by the sacrifice of His death all the sins of the world have been expiated.

Comment on Colossians 1: 14

71.   For although it is true that we must not try to decide what is God's will by prying into His secret counsel, when He has made it plain to us by external signs, yet that does not mean that God has not determined secretly within Himself what He wishes to do with every single man.

But I pass from that point which is not relevant to the present context, for the apostle's meaning here is simply that no nation of the earth and no rank of society is excluded from salvation, since God wills to offer the Gospel to all without exception...For as there is one God, the Creator and Father of all, so, he declares, there is one Mediator, through whom access to God is not given only to one nation, or to few men of a particular class, but to all, for the benefit of the sacrifice, by which He has expiated for our sins, applies to all...The universal term 'all' must always be referred to classes of men but never to individuals. It is as if he had said, 'Not only Jews, but also Greeks, not only people of humble rank but also princes have been redeemed by the death of Christ.' Since therefore He intends the benefit of His death to be common to all, those who hold a view that would exclude any from the hope of salvation do Him an injury.

Comment on 1 Timothy 2: 3-5

72.   ...no one unless deprived of sense and judgement can believe that salvation is ordained in the secret counsel of God equally for all...Who does not see that the reference [1 Tim. 2:4] is to orders of men rather than individual men? Nor indeed does the distinction lack substantial ground: what is meant is not individuals of nations but nations of individuals. At any rate, the context makes it clear that no other will of God is intended than that which appears in the external preaching of the Gospel. Thus Paul means that God wills the salvation of all whom He mercifully invites by the preaching of Christ.

Concerning the Eternal Predestination of God, 109

73.   So then, seeing it is God his will that all men should be partakers of that salvation which he hath sent in the person of his only begotten Son...yet we must mark that Saint Paul speaketh not here of every particular man, but of all sorts, and of all people: Therefore, when he saith, that God will

34

have all men to be saved, we must not think that he speaketh here of Peter, or John, but his meaning is this, that whereas in times past he chose out one certain people for himself, he meaneth now to show mercy to all the world...but when Jesus Christ came to be a common Saviour for all in general, he offered the grace of God his father, to the end that all might receive it...Let us see now, whether God will draw all the world to [the Gospel] or not. No, no: for then had our Lord Jesus Christ said in vain No man can come to me, unless God my Father teach him (Jn. 6:44)...

It followeth then, that before the world was made, (as Saint Paul saith in the first to the Ephesians) God chose such as it pleased him: and it pertaineth not to us to know, why this man, more than that man, we know not the reason...Saint Paul speaketh not here of every particular man, (as we shewed already) but he speaketh of all people...now God showeth himself a Saviour of all the world...Saint Paul speaketh not in this place, of the strait counsell of God, neither that he meaneth to lead us to this everlasting election & choice which was before the beginning of the world, but only sheweth us what God his will and pleasure is, so far forth as we may know it. Truth it is, that God changeth not, neither hath he two wills, neither does he use any counterfeit dealing, as though he meant one thing, but would not have it so. And yet doth the Scripture speak unto us after two sorts touching the will of God...God doeth exhort all men generally, thereby we may judge, that it is the will of God, that all men should be saved, as he saith also by the Prophet Ezekiel I will not the death of a sinner, but that he turn himself and live (Ezek. 18:23)...For Jesus Christ is not a Saviour of three or four, but he offereth himself to all...And is he not the Saviour of the whole world as well? Is Jesus Christ come to be the Mediator between two or three men only? No, no: but he is the Mediator between God and men...

Sermons on Timothy and Titus, 149-60

74.   Repentance and faith must needs go together...God receiveth us to mercy, and daily pardoneth our faults through his free goodness: and that we be justified because Jesus Christ hath reconciled him unto us, inasmuch as he accepteth us for righteous though we be wretched sinners: in preaching this, it behoveth us to add, how it is upon condition that we return unto God: as was spoken of heretofore by the prophets.

Sermons on Timothy and Titus, 1181-2

75.   Indeed the death of Christ was life for the whole world...

Comment on Hebrews 8: 2

76.   He suffered death in the common way of men, but He made divine atonement for the sins of the world as a Priest.

Comment on Hebrews 8: 4

77.   To bear the sins means to free those who have sinned from their guilt by his satisfaction. He says many meaning all, as in Rom. 5:15. It is of course certain that not all enjoy the fruits of Christ's death, but this happens because their unbelief hinders them.

Comment on Hebrews 9: 27

78.   He brought His own blood into the heavenly sanctuary in order to atone for the sins of the world.

Comment on Hebrews 13: 12

79.   So we must beware, or souls redeemed by Christ may perish by our carelessness, for their salvation to some degree was put into our hands by God.

Comment on James 5: 20

80.   It was not a common or a small favour that God put off the manifestation of Christ to their

time, when He had ordained Him by His eternal counsel for the salvation of the world...a remedy for mankind...He ordained that Christ should be the Redeemer, who would deliver the lost race of man from ruin...[but] the manifestation of Christ does not refer to all indiscriminately, but belongs only to those whom He illumines by the Gospel.

Comment on 1 Peter 1: 20

81.   We have the Gospel in its entirety, when we know that He who had long been promised as Redeemer came down from heaven, put on our flesh, lived in the world, experienced death and then rose again; and secondly when we see the purpose and fruits of all these things in the fact that He was God with us, that He gave us in Himself a sure pledge of our adoption, that by the grace of His Spirit He has cleansed us from the stains of our carnal iniquities and consecrated us to be temples to God, that He has raised us from the depths to heaven, that by His sacrificial death He has made atonement for the sins of the world, that He has reconciled us to the Father, and that He has been the source of righteousness and life for us. Whoever holds to these things has rightly grasped the Gospel.

Comment on 2 Peter 1: 16

82.   Christ redeemed us to have us as a people separated from all the iniquities of the world, devoted to holiness and purity. Those who throw over the traces and plunge themselves into every kind of licence are not unjustly said to deny Christ, by whom they were redeemed.

Comment on 2 Peter 2: 1

83.   This is His wondrous love towards the human race, that He desires all men to be saved, and is prepared to bring even the perishing to safety...It could be asked here, if God does not want any to perish, why do so many in fact perish? My reply is that no mention is made here of the secret decree of God by which the wicked are doomed to their own ruin, but only of His loving-kindness as it is made known to us in the Gospel. There God stretches out His hand to all alike, but He only grasps those (in such a way as to lead to Himself) whom He has chosen before the foundation of the world.

Comment on 2 Peter 3: 9

84.   He put this in for amplification, that believers might be convinced that the expiation made by Christ extends to all who by faith embrace the Gospel. But here the question may be asked as to how the sins of the whole world have been expiated. I pass over the dreams of the fanatics, who make this a reason to extend salvation to all the reprobate and even to Satan himself. Such a monstrous idea is not worth refuting. Those who want to avoid this absurdity have said that Christ suffered sufficiently for the whole world but effectively only for the elect. This solution has commonly prevailed in the schools. Although I allow the truth of this, I deny that it fits the passage. For John's purpose was only to make this blessing common to the whole church. Therefore, under the word 'all' he does not include the reprobate, but refers to all who would believe and those who were scattered through various regions of the earth. For, as is meet, the grace of Christ is really made clear when it is declared to be the only salvation of the world.

Comment on 1 John 2: 2

85.   Georgius thinks he argues very acutely when he says: Christ is the propitiation for the sins of the whole world; and hence those who wish to exclude the reprobate from participation in Christ must place them outside the world. For this, the common solution does not avail, that Christ suffered sufficiently for all, but efficaciously only for the elect. By this great absurdity, this monk has sought applause in his own fraternity, but it has no weight with me. Wherever the faithful are dispersed throughout the world, John [1 Jn. 2:2] extends to them the expiation wrought by Christ's

death. But this does not alter the fact that the reprobate are mixed up with the elect in the world. It is incontestable that Christ came for the expiation of the sins of the whole world. But the solution lies close at hand, that whosoever believes in Him should not perish but should have eternal life (Jn. 3:15). For the present question is not how great the power of Christ is or what efficacy it has in itself, but to whom He gives Himself to be enjoyed. If possession lies in faith and faith emanates from the Spirit of adoption, it follows that only he is reckoned in the number of God's children who will be a partaker of Christ. The evangelist John sets forth the office of Christ as nothing else than by His death to gather the children of God into one (Jn. 11:52). Hence, we conclude that, though reconciliation is offered to all through Him, yet the benefit is peculiar to the elect, that they may be gathered into the society of life. However, while I say it is offered to all, I do not mean that this embassy, by which on Paul's testimony (2 Cor. 5:18) God reconciles the world to Himself, reaches to all, but that it is not sealed indiscriminately on the hearts of all to whom it comes so as to be effectual.

Concerning the Eternal Predestination of God, 148-9

86. He again shows the cause of Christ's coming and His office when he says that He was sent to be the propitiation for sins...For propitiation strictly refers to the sacrifice of His death. Hence we see that to Christ alone belongs this honour of expiating for the sins of the world and taking away the enmity between God and us.

Comment on 1 John 4: 10

87. Certainly, in 2 Pet. 2:1, there is reference only to Christ, and He is called Master there. Denying...Christ, he says, of those who have been redeemed by His blood, and now enslave themselves again to the devil, frustrating (as best they may) that incomparable boon.

Comment on Jude 4

88. [Him God set forth to be a propitiation through faith in his blood for our sins, and not for ours only, but also for the sins of the whole world...But though he died for all, all do not receive the benefit of his death, but those only to whom the merit of his passion is communicated... *(Articles III, IV of the Sixth Session of the Council of Trent)]*

The third and fourth heads I do not touch...

Antidote to the Council of Trent
Tracts, iii. 93, 109

89. ...Christ, who is the salvation of the world,...

Catechism of the Church of Geneva,
Tracts, ii. 47

90. I John Calvin, servant of the Word of God in the church of Geneva, weakened by many illnesses...thank God that he has not only shown mercy to me, his poor creature...and suffered me in all sins and weaknesses, but what is more than that, he has made me a partaker of his grace to serve him through my work...I confess to live and die in this faith which he has given me, inasmuch as I have no other hope or refuge than his predestination upon which my entire salvation is grounded. I embrace the grace which he has offered me in our Lord Jesus Christ, and accept the merits of his suffering and dying that through him all my sins are buried; and I humbly beg him to wash me and cleanse me with the blood of our great Redeemer, as it was shed for all poor sinners so that I, when I appear before his face, may bear his likeness.

Calvin's Last Will (April 25, 1564)
Letters of John Calvin, 29

Moïse Amyraut
(1596-1664)

Appendix I

See Roger Nicole, 'John Calvin's view of the extent of the Atonement', *Westminster Theological Journal* 47 (1985), 197-225

In this detailed and closely-reasoned article, the author attempts to demonstrate that Calvin's theology of redemption is consistent with the doctrine of limited atonement. By classifying and clarifying Calvin's various statements, the author seeks to invalidate the Amyraldian interpretation of Calvin's thought. The following are replies to Nicole's thirteen concluding arguments against a dualistic universal/particular view of Calvin's theology (220ff).

Note: To facilitate ready access to the Calvin quotations, Calvinus numbering is used, e.g. *Comm. 2 Pet. 3:9* is *#83*.

1.   *Nicole*: 'The strong structure of Calvin's theology in terms of the divine purpose does appear to imply this specific [definite atonement] reference. It seems difficult to imagine that Calvin would posit as the purpose of Christ an indefinite, hypothetical redemption, when at so many other points it is plainly apparent that the specific elective purpose of God is the controlling feature of his outlook.'

Reply: Contrary to Nicole's unbalanced view, Calvin does combine an 'indefinite' hypothetical redemption for all with a 'definite' application to the elect (#18, 21, 22, 49, 64, 67, 74). Calvin's dualistic view correlates with his acceptance of the paradox of the secret/revealed will distinction. The elective purpose is not the controlling feature of Calvin's outlook: when a text of Scripture demands it, he asserts the two aspects of the paradox evenly (see #83). Nicole invalidly imputes to Calvin his own scholastic perspective.

2.   *Nicole*: '...To assume a hypothetical redemptive purpose more inclusive that the election of grace is doing precisely what [Calvin] precludes. It is difficult to assume that Calvin would open himself to such self-contradiction.'

Reply: Concerning ultimate and hypothetical divine purposes, what Nicole regards as a 'self-contradiction' - an instance of scholastic impatience - is both acknowledged and answered by Calvin according to his dualistic methodology (see #27, 73).

3.   *Nicole*: '...What Christ has accomplished on the cross is not so much to secure the salvability of all humans, as actually to accomplish the salvation of those whom he does redeem.'

Reply: Calvin asserts both the 'salvability of all' and the actual salvation of the elect. Again, according to his dualistic methodology, Calvin insists that while the application is for the elect, the cross makes 'potential' provision for all (without using the term). Faith is evidence of election: the 'us' are those who believe. But the antecedent provision is broader in scope than the number of the elect (see #19, 64, 66, 67).

4.   *Nicole*: 'Calvin, as well as the Scripture itself, frequently conjoins in the same sentence certain

benefits which accrue only to the elect...'

Reply: Of course only the elect actually receive the benefits of redemption. This is not contested. The applied efficacy of the cross is ensured by the secret will of God. Yet Calvin recognises a broader provision of redemptive grace according to God's revealed will (see #58, 77).

5.   *Nicole*: 'Calvin, following Scripture, conjoins closely the [extent of the] priestly work of Christ in his substitutionary death with [the extent of] his priestly work as intercessor.' (Against R. T. Kendall who argued that the former was unlimited and the latter limited).

Reply: It is perfectly plain, contra Kendall and Nicole, that the same dualism which applies to Christ's death also applies to his intercession. They are indeed coextensive, but in Calvin's dualistic sense (see #51).

6.   *Nicole*: 'Calvin deals with texts which are usually associated with a universal saving intent in a way which shows that he was mindful at that very moment of the elective purpose of God.'

Reply: Calvin's comments on the cited texts (Ezek. 18:32, John 3:16, 2 Pet. 3:9) simply reveal his use of the secret/revealed will distinction to explain how a general provision is restricted in application (see #21-22, 45, 83). Regarding 1 Tim. 2:4-6, Nicole (like many others) misconstrues Calvin's intent entirely. Quite contrary to Nicole's remarks, Calvin - unlike Augustine and Owen - explicitly denies that Paul is concerned with elect individuals according to God's secret will. While Calvin insists - arguably in this immediate context - that 'all' must be expounded as racial and social groups - a universalism of kinds - yet, since he believes Paul has God's revealed will in mind, redemptive provision is not denied to any individual members of each group (see #71, 72, 73, also 18). Likewise, Calvin's own 'all' in *Comm. Rom. 5:18* (#58) clearly refers to individuals rather than classes or groups, otherwise, he would contradict his universalism of kinds. Furthermore, when Calvin is commenting on the meaning of 'world' vis-a-vis Jewish nationalism in *Comm. John 1:29* (#44), his generic remarks clearly embrace individuals of each racial group. 'Each' can only mean 'each individual' rather than 'each nation'. In short, unlike Owen and others, Calvin does not in these passages expound 'world' and 'all' to mean 'some of each nation' since God's revealed will is in view. On the other hand, where the secret efficacious will is implied as in *Comm. Zeph. 3:9*, Calvin takes 'all' to mean 'some'. This however does not apply to the other passages in question.

Nicole writes (ibid): 'Now we have never met an upholder of universal atonement who would favour such an interpretation', i.e. Nicole's understanding of Calvin on 1 Tim. 2: 4-6. However, Augustine is an illustrious example, whose exegesis of the passage Calvin is thought to have followed (see 'Enchiridion', *Writings of the Nicene and Post-Nicene Fathers*, Schaff edition (1887), iii. 270). On the atonement, Augustine wrote: 'For it is good for all men to hear [Christ's] voice and live, by passing to the life of godliness from the death of ungodliness. Of this death the Apostle Paul says, "Therefore all are dead, and He died for all, that they which live should not henceforth live unto themselves, but unto Him which died for them and rose again." (2 Cor. 5:14-15). Thus all, without one exception, were dead in sins, whether original or voluntary sins, sins of ignorance, or sins committed against knowledge; and for all the dead there died the only one person who lived, that is, who had no sin whatever, in order that they who live by the remission of their sins should live, not to themselves, but to Him who died for all, for our sins, and rose again for our justification...' (*The City of God*, Works, ed. M. Dods (1872), ii. 354).

Richard Baxter's comment on Augustine is relevant here: 'As for Augustine and some Protestants, they oft deny that Christ redeemeth any but the faithful, because the word redemption is ambiguous, and sometimes taken for the price or ransom paid, and often for the very liberation of the captive sinner. And when Austin denieth common redemption, he taketh redemption in this last sense, for actual deliverance. But he asserteth it in the first sense, that Christ died for all. Yea, he thought his death is actually applied to the true justification and sanctification of some reprobates that fall away and perish, though the elect only are so redeemed and saved. Read yourself Augustine...and you will see this with your own eyes' (*Catholick Theologie*, 1675, II. 57-8; quoted in my *Atonement and Justification,* 91).

Seemingly consistent with Augustine before him and certainly with Baxter after him, Calvin did teach universal grace (see #10, 37, 49, 58).

7.   *Nicole*: 'The embarrassment which some of Calvin's universal expressions may cause the upholder of definite atonement may be alleviated by the consideration that Calvin meant to place special emphasis on the indiscriminate call of the gospel. It is certainly in this sense that Calvin himself interprets 2 Pet. 3: 9 and the same hermeneutic may apply to his own statements.'

Reply: Those who agree with Calvin feel no such embarrassment, a fact which speaks for itself. For those who think differently, Nicole's 'alleviation' is illusory, and only possible at the expense of vital Calvin evidence. Although no reference is made to the atonement in *Comm. 2 Pet.* 3:9 (#83), Calvin obviously sees universal atonement as the prerequisite of the universal offer in *Comm. Rom. 5:18* (#58) and *Sermons on Ephesians*, p. 684-5 (#69). In short, Nicole's 'hermenuetic' relies upon a distortion of authentic Calvinism.

8.   *Nicole*: 'There are in Scripture as well as in Calvin passages where the particular intent of Christ's death is stressed,' viz. Matt. 1:21, John 10:15, John 15:13, Acts 20:28, Eph. 5:23-6, and Titus 2:14.

Reply: These passages do not support the exclusive particularism Nicole and others subscribe to. To do so, they would have to say 'Christ died only for his people, his sheep, his friends, his church and for us'. But none of the cited texts say this. They are perfectly consistent with Amyraut's efficacious particularism: 'Christ's intention was to die for all men in respect of the sufficiency of his satisfaction, but for the elect only in respect of its quickening and saving virtue and efficacy' (Quick, *Synodicon*, ii. 354). Calvin's ubiquitous redemptive dualism clearly conforms to this and his comments on the texts in question say nothing otherwise.

In his comment on Matt. 1:21 (#24), Calvin notes the Jewish significance of 'his people', after which he notes the universal promise of salvation. This is a far cry from Owen's exclusively particularist exegesis of the verse (see *The Death of Death, Works*, x. 209). Regarding John 10:15, Christ is simply contrasting what he is prepared to do for the sheep with the cowardice of the false shepherds, viz. 'They don't care for the sheep, but I will die for them'. The question of extent is not the issue, neither does Calvin's comment touch on this. In his comment on John 15:13, Calvin actually refers the reader to John 3, where his comments are 'embarrassingly' universalist (see #45, 57)! Calvin's comment on Acts 20: 28 (#54) surely heightens the embarrassment. The text occasioned one of several statements where Calvin allows the possibility of some perishing for whom Christ died. His language is utterly at odds with the theory of limited atonement (see also #12, 55, 60, 68, 69, 79, 87).

The observations made on John 10:15 also apply to Eph. 5: 23-6. This is not a proof-text for limited atonement and, unlike Owen, Calvin nowhere exploits it to that end. Paul's statement merely illustrates the sacrificial quality of Christ's love rather than its extent, and Calvin's comment reflects this concern. In Titus 2:14, Paul is concerned simply with the sanctifying impact of Christ's death for 'us' who believe, and Calvin's comment stresses this specific point accordingly.

9.   *Nicole*: 'Calvin's statement in response to Heshusius...appears to be a categorical denial of universal atonement.'

Reply: I have discussed Calvin's response to Heshusius in the introduction and in Atonement and Justification, p. 87. If Nicole and others find it impossible to regard Calvin as a universalist, it is surely statistically illogical for them to 'alleviate their embarrassment' by explaining away his typical universalist language on the strength of one apparently particularist statement. This will not do, quite apart from casting aspersions on Calvin's obvious claim to some semblance of logical consistency! I believe my solution explains how Calvin's admittedly problematic statement is to be understood.

10.   *Nicole*: 'Calvin follows Scripture in the terms he commonly uses to describe the atoning work of Christ: 'Reconciliation,' 'redemption,' 'propitiation.' To these may be added the term 'satisfaction,' not found per se in Scripture, but commonly used by theologians. All these terms connate an accomplishment that actually transforms the relationship between God and the sinner...The language of Calvin does not fit a mere potential blessing which remains ineffective pending some performance by the sinner, which would then make it truly operative...'

Reply: Nicole's comments on the terms 'reconciliation', 'redemption', 'propitiation' and 'satisfaction' reflect the inhibitions of scholastic high orthodoxy rather than Calvin himself. Only ignorance of the reformer's repeated and explicit statements could enable Nicole to deny that Calvin believed in something akin to 'potential' as well as 'received' grace. While Calvin insists that repentance and faith are the results of special (or 'received'?) grace in the hearts of the elect (*Inst*. II. ii. 6), this qualification is not always present when he highlights unbelief as the factor hindering the personal enjoyment of salvation. Like Paul who taught that faith is a duty as well as a gift, Calvin clearly taught that a 'potentially available' salvation is hindered by unbelief (see #16, 18, 44, 49, 58, 67, 77).

11.   *Nicole*: '...Christ on the cross underwent the divine penalty which God would otherwise inflict on the sinner. Who does not see that if this is so, and if the atonement is universal, no one will be punished at the last judgement?'

Reply: Whether Nicole likes it or not, Calvin's commitment to the concept of penal substitution did not involve a high orthodox theory of definite atonement (see #20, 77, 86). He never subscribed to the 'double payment' doctrine of Beza. Calvin even declares that unbelievers are 'doubly culpable' for rejecting salvation (see #11, 17, 18, 20). Indeed, unbelievers are guilty of rejecting nothing if nothing was provided for them. On this, Calvin is quite clear (#16).

12.   *Nicole*: 'Calvin's strong trinitarian view would certainly lead him to recognize a unity of purpose between the three persons of the Godhead...But universal atonement introduces a fundamental disjunction between the universal intent of the Son, who gave himself for all and the particular purpose of the Father who elected only some people, and of the Holy Spirit, who confers

regeneration, faith and repentance to the elect only. Here again it is difficult to imagine that Calvin would remain unaware of such a fatal flaw at the heart of his theology.'

Reply: Regarding Calvin's trinitarianism, there is not the disjunction between the universal intent of the Son and the particular intent of the Father imagined by Nicole. True, Calvin taught that the efficacy of an otherwise universal atonement is guaranteed by the Holy Spirit's work. However, Calvin evidently taught that the persons of the trinity concur in redeeming actvity, each in a dualistic way. The Father reaches out to all while only grasping the elect (#83); the Son redeems all sufficiently but only the elect effectually (#42); the Holy Spirit bestows 'regeneration only on the elect' while still 'touching the reprobate with a taste of his grace' (Comm. Heb. 6:4-5). Contrary to Nicole's fears, Calvin's teaching seems quite flawless on this point!

13.   *Nicole*: 'A historical difficulty appears when we attempt to explain how Reformed thought moved so quickly away from Calvin's alleged endorsement of universal atonement...can we really accept that [Beza's] influence was so very far-reaching that he practically single-handedly reverted the whole trend in Reformed circles, putting himself at loggerheads not only with Calvin, but as it is alleged, with Scripture itself?'

Reply: Where is the historical difficulty of admitting that Beza and Reformed orthodoxy moved away from Calvin's balanced biblicism? It is not uncommon in all spheres of human thought for disciples to adopt more extreme positions than their masters. As with the disciples of Arminius, so with Calvin's 'official' followers. On the basis of recent research, none can question that Beza taught a rigorous doctrine of limited atonement, using language not found in Calvin. Embarrassed by the implications of this, high orthodox scholars have resorted to a theory of doctrinal development to reconcile Calvin and Beza. Thus Calvin's doctrine has been described as 'undeveloped' by later standards. As a consequence, the Amyraldians, whilst claiming to perpetuate authentic Calvinism, were charged with heresy because they opposed what they saw as the 'over-developed' formulations of high orthodox theologians. In short, questionable perspectives created confusion! It is clear therefore, in view of the unrecognized cogency of Amyraut's case, that high orthodoxy was a distortion of Calvin's theology. In consequence, it remains for the opponents of Amyraldianism to renounce Calvin also rather than pretend that his theology coincides with theirs. Contrary to Nicole's conclusion, one must affirm that a dualistic account of redemption fits better than a theory of limited, particular grace into the total pattern of Calvin's teaching. As for the foundations of Calvin's teaching, A. N. S. Lane's conclusion provides an accurate evaluation:

Calvin was above all a biblical theologian...His constant involvement with the biblical text, together with his aversion to speculation beyond what is revealed, kept him from abandoning some of the genuine biblical tensions and paradoxes...Calvin was prepared to recognise both God's universal love for all mankind and his desire for all to repent and his purpose that some only should be saved. To the feeble human mind these are irreconcilable. The mark of the true disciple of Calvin is his willingness to accept biblical paradox and not to seek to reconcile it in the direction of one pole or the other. ('The Quest for the Historical Calvin', *Evangelical Quarterly* 55.2 (1983), 113).

Postscript:
(a) A standard objection to the Amyraldian view is that if any perish for whom Christ died, then His blood was 'wasted' or shed in vain and thus God's saving will is 'frustrated'. This objection never troubled Calvin. His three levels of love statement (#8) is relevant here: whereas special love is efficacious, general love is not.

Also, do not apostates despise and waste the blood of Christ (Heb. 10: 29)? Exegetically, where is the problem? In view of 2 Pet. 2: 1 and Jude 4, Calvin affirms that even apostates were 'redeemed by Christ' (#82, 87). This does not affect the certain salvation of the elect. God's secret will is never frustrated even though His revealed will often is (Matt. 22: 5; Acts 7: 51). Calvin admits the possibility that 'the price of the blood of Christ is wasted' (#59). He clearly acknowledges this 'frustration' (#87). With respect to unbelievers, Calvin allows for the work of Christ being 'useless' (#7) and 'spurned' (#49).

(b) The objection 'that the sins of all cannot be propitiated if God's wrath remains on those who are eternally damned' is met by Calvin. He acknowledges that we are loved and hated simultaneously, so to speak. In his exposition of Rom. 5: 10, Calvin says, 'note the double aspect'. This surely makes sense of Jn. 3: 16 and 36, where God declares a love even for unbelievers on whom His wrath abides. While they live, there is hope. Even believers, as Calvin makes clear, are under divine wrath until they believe, notwithstanding God's secret counsel effectually to save them. The propitiation available for all is not theirs until they believe. Calvin clearly implies this understanding (see #18-20, 77, 83).

(c) A. A. Hodge's criticism of the Amyraldian view is often cited, that 'God loves all men sufficiently to give them his Son to die for them, but not loving them enough to give them faith and repentance' (*The Atonement*, 1868, 349). However, this remark is more consistent with hypercalvinism than 'free offer' high Calvinism and may be turned against the author and his school thus: 'God loves all men sufficiently to offer his Son to them, but not enough actually to save them'. (See Iain H. Murray, 'Richard Baxter - the Reluctant Puritan?' in *Advancing in Adversity* (Westminster Conference, 1991), 9.) For all its 'wit', this objection is a caricature of both Amyraldianism *and* the love of God. It ignores the balancing consideration of human wilfulness generally ignored by hypercalvinists.

(d) Dr Richard Muller concedes that Calvin's successors were more scholastic in method than the reformer. He even admits they were 'more rationalistic' (*Christ and the Decree*, 1988, 12). However, he is careful to point out that Calvin, notwithstanding his strongly-expressed aversion to scholasticism in general, was not totally opposed to such modes of thought ('Calvin and the "Calvinists": Assessing Continuities and Discontinuities between the Reformation and Orthodoxy', *Calvin Theological Journal* 31 (1996), 125-60). But despite Muller's attempts to argue continuity between Calvin and his successors, he fails to close the gap on the question of the extent of the atonement. He acknowledges that Calvin distinguished between the universalist and particular aspects of Christ's work, insisting that the reformer employs a distinction between what is 'unlimited' in 'fullness' and what is 'limited' in 'actuality' (*Christ and the Decree*, 34). Incidentally, this is the very kind of distinction affirmed by Amyraut but denied by many of the Reformed scholastics. While Muller agrees that Calvin's use of 'satisfaction' and 'expiation' connotes 'unlimited atonement', he argues that the reformer uses 'reconciliation' and 'redemption' in respect of 'limited atonement' (Ibid). There is confusion here. Calvin clearly uses *all* these terms to express 'benefits' available to all but only 'actually' enjoyed by the elect. Surprisingly, Muller fails to document his claims. The simple fact is that Calvin clearly used 'reconciliation' and 'redemption' in a universal sense, as a few brief specimens will show (see Calvinus, #25, 50, 52, 53, 57). Furthermore, regarding Muller's insistence that a 'hypothetical' dimension to the atonement is 'superfluous' (Ibid), such a view is obviously not shared by Calvin who clearly taught that the benefits of Christ's death are available to all *if* only they believe (see *Calvinus*, #77). If Muller fails, at the outset, convincingly to demonstrate Calvin's affinity with later Reformed orthodoxy, his thesis that 'the master' was part of its development is as doubtful as the scholastic cause is flawed from a truly *sola scriptura* standpoint. Elsewhere, he concedes that 'Calvin's teaching was ... capable of being cited with significant effect by Moyse Amyraut against his Reformed opponents' (*The Unaccommodated Calvin*, 2000, 62).

Appendix II

See Jonathan H. Rainbow, *The Will of God and the Cross* (Pickwick Publications 1990).

In this rigorously argued and well documented work, the author defends the thesis that John Calvin held the doctrine of limited redemption. Placing the reformer within an historical theological context covering the 4th-16th centuries, we are told that Augustine, Gottschalk, Wyclif, Hus, Bucer and others all subscribed to limited atonement. The author attempts to demonstrate that Calvin simply perpetuated this theological tradition. In the process, he seeks to purge from our understanding of Calvin all traces of Amyraldianism: 'To be blunt, there is a need to get Amyraut out of the picture' (p. 8). This preoccupation is reflected in Dr Rainbow's conclusion: 'Under whatever label, John Calvin, as a limited redemptionist, belongs historically with Augustine, Gottschalk, Bucer, Beza, and Reformed orthodoxy - not with Amyraut' (p. 185). The unanswered question is how are we to understand Amyraut's claim to be a faithful disciple of Calvin?

The author commences his case by placing Calvin firmly in the Augustinian tradition. We are told that for Augustine, the omnipotence of God is the ruling motif. This rules out the idea that God wills anything which is not effectual: 'God always and actually does what he wills' (p. 10). Thus the idea of an indefinite, hypothetical redemption is ruled out: 'Whom God wills to save through the death of Christ, he does in fact save, and so the intent of Christ's sacrifice can be measured by the result' (p. 11).

However, the evidence cited is not convincing. We are told that 'The limitation of redemption to the elect appeared occasionally in Augustine in contexts where the doctrine of Christ's death was not the principal topic. In one sense, such offhand remarks are a more revealing witness to his belief in limited redemption than are the longer texts which will be examined shortly...'(ibid). According to this criterion, the 'offhand' Calvinus evidence challenges Rainbow's perception of Calvin, thus raising initial doubts about Calvin's dependence on Augustine. Baxter's very different perception of Augustine is relevant at this point (see above). As for the author's citations, they do not demonstrate his case: when Augustine - commenting on Christ's good shepherd discourse (Jn. 10) - says that unbelieving Jews 'are not won to eternal life by the price of [Christ's] own blood', he merely says they were 'not won', not that the sheep were 'alone died for'. Likewise he says that '[Christ] and only he was the purchaser', not that 'the sheep and they alone were died for'. Another citation merely proves the efficacy of redemption rather than a limited divine redemptive intent.

Regarding Augustine's treatment of the 'all' and 'world' texts of Scripture, the author claims that a 'two worlds' (elect and reprobate) concept underlies Augustine's approach. But where does Calvin adopt this view? Calvin's comment on John 17:9 (#51) is no proof at all. Although John Owen was to follow Augustine's 'elect world' view of 2 Cor. 5:19, Calvin never did. For all the similarities between Augustine and Calvin over 1 John 2:2, the latter never adopted the universal rule that 'whole world' means 'the church'.

Contrary to the author's claim, the difference between Augustine's and Calvin's exegesis of the divine will in 1 Tim. 2:4-6 could not be more fundamental: whereas Augustine insists that it is an effectual rather than a conditional will, Calvin believed the reverse. While Calvin agrees that Paul speaks of a 'universalism of kinds', his revealed will exegesis means something quite different from Augustine's. Calvin clearly states that 'nations of individuals' rather than 'individuals of nations' are intended. Hence, unlike Augustine, Calvin clearly taught that a redemptive provision is offered to such individuals in general and not merely to the elect (see #67, 71, 72, 73).

These criticisms have serious implications for the overall cogency of Rainbow's case. If the Augustinian exegesis of 1 Tim. 2 is fundamental to the limited redemptionist thesis, and if Calvin was not in fact 'a completely loyal and unoriginal Augustinian' as Rainbow claims (p. 136), then his attempt to invalidate 'Amyraut's viewpoint' (p. 143) becomes questonable to say the least.

Turning to the medieval period of the debate, the author traces the influence of the Augustinian legacy. While Augustine's disciple Prosper of Aquitaine pursued a more 'attenuated' position than his master, the 9th century Gottschalk plainly adopted an ultra-Augustinian stance. While Prosper clearly anticipated Calvin and Amyraut, Rainbow is incorrect to assume that Gottschalk did (p. 29). Indeed, linking the extent of redemption to its nature was certainly a feature of Beza but not of Calvin. For *Prosper, see Prosper of Aquitaine; Defence of St Augustine*, tr. P. de Letter (1963), 150, 164).

Coming to the scholastic period, one questions the accuracy of Rainbow's portrayal of Thomas Aquinas and his influence. Since he 'sacrificed the Augustinian axiom that God's will to save must always be effectual' (p. 36), we are told that Aquinas' sufficiency-efficiency distinction made him the precursor of Amyraut rather than Calvin. However, Rainbow's attempt to drive a wedge between Calvin and Amyraut on this issue is out of order. He ignores the fact that Calvin clearly accepted the sufficiency-efficiency distinction (see #19, 42, 84). He did not 'sweep the discussion clean' of this particular 'device' (p. 46). Furthermore, Aquinas' understanding of this found clear expression in the *Canons of Trent*, a formulation Calvin was evidently quite happy with (#88). One is not impressed by Rainbow's dismissal of this evidence (p. 149), although it is obviously important to him to play down any parallels between Calvin and Amyraut.

Rainbow's attempt to include Wyclif and Hus in the strict limited redemptionist tradition is not very peruasive, and his conclusion that 'Calvin's doctrine of the extent of redemption would be a return to that of Gottschalk and Augustine' is simply wide of the mark. In addition, his remarks on the use of the term 'scholastic' lack discrimination. To say 'Amyraut has a better claim to it than Beza' (p. 48) is question begging. It is arguable that since Beza was an Aristotelian scholastic, then perhaps, like Calvin, Amyraut was influenced by Thomistic ideas. However, as Armstrong proves beyond all doubt, from the perspective of a revived Aristotelianism within Reformed orthodoxy, Amyraut was not a scholastic theologian.

Coming to Calvin's contemporaries, the author's chapter on Martin Bucer and the Anabaptists is interesting and enlightening. In rejecting anabaptist universalism, Bucer clearly taught a very explicit doctrine of limited redemption. Augustinian and Gottschalkian elements are very evident in Bucer's thought. Without questioning Bucer's obvious general influence on Calvin, Rainbow fails to prove that 'the limited redemptionist tradition was hand-delivered, as it were, to John Calvin' (p. 61). Unlike Bucer, Calvin did not teach a limited satisfaction (#17, 18, 20, 77). Unlike Bucer, Calvin does not equate 'the world' with 'the elect' (#45). Notwithstanding his debt to Bucer's commentary on Romans, Calvin clearly rejected Bucer's limited redemptionist views in his comment on Rom. 5: 18 (#58). It seems rather significant that Rainbow nowhere cites this key piece of evidence. In view of Bucer's unambiguous position, it is all the more remarkable that Calvin did not agree with it. He clearly had some sympathy with the anabaptist case. Again, Rainbow fails in his attempt (p. 63) to distance Calvin from Amyraut. Calvin clearly displayed that independence of mind for which he was famous. Indeed, as 'the Amyraut thesis implies', Calvin 'simply went a different way'.

Turning to Rainbow's discussion of Calvin's theology, it becomes clear that he - rather than 'the Saumur professor' - is distorting the reformer's thought. In his discussion of the trinitarian context of Calvin's views on election and redemption, Rainbow is guilty of gross misrepresentation of Amyraut. Recognizing Amyraut's dualistic conception of the will of God, viz. God desires the salvation of all conditionally but only the elect absolutely, Rainbow then says: 'The pivotal point in all this is that Amyraut linked the death of Christ to the general saving will of God and not to the electing will of God' (p. 70). Rainbow is clearly unaware of Amyraut's statement made at the National Synod of Alençon (1637) where he declared 'That Jesus Christ died for all men sufficiently, but for the elect only effectually: and that consequently his intention was to die for all men in respect of the sufficiency of his satisfaction, but for the elect only in respect of its quickening and saving virtue and efficacy; which is to say, that Christ's will was that the sacrifice of his cross should be of an infinite price and value, and most abundantly sufficient to expiate the sins of the whole world; yet nevertheless the efficacy of his death appertains only unto the elect...' (Quick, *Synodicon*, ii. 354). Thus, contrary to Rainbow's charge, Amyraut taught that the death of Christ was linked to both aspects of the divine will.

Amyraut clearly derived his dualistic distinctive from Calvin, and Rainbow's attempts to minimize this are without foundation (p. 71). As Calvin argued that God's will is 'one and simple' (*Inst.* 1. xviii. 3), so Amyraut agreed that 'Certainly the will of God is only one and of a supremely simple nature' (Armstrong, p. 194). When Calvin argued that the apparent duality of the divine will was due to the imperfection of human perception, Amyraut likewise said that God's will 'ought to be considered in two ways - according to our weak manner of conceiving' (Ibid). Whether or not Amyraut was guilty of using this dualistic device as a tool for a systematic theology, he could justly claim - unlike Beza - that his method was derived from Calvin.

Rainbow then asks: 'The crucial question here is whether in Calvin's theology the saving work of Christ was linked to the particular saving purpose of God the Father. Amyraut said no...' (p. 71). Again, Amyraut's own words are a sufficient answer: '...this was the most free counsel and gracious purpose both of God the Father, in giving his Son for the salvation of mankind, and of the Lord Jesus Christ, in suffering the pains of death, that the efficacy thereof should particularly belong unto all the elect, and to them only, to give them justifying faith, and by it to bring them infallibly unto salvation, and thus effectually to redeem all those and none other, who were from all eternity from among all people, nations and tongues, chosen unto salvation' (Quick, op. cit., p. 354; see also Armstrong, p. 199). Rainbow's further question, 'But was Amyraut actually following Calvin?' may be answered thus: both Calvin and Amyraut taught that the 'harmonious and connected work of the Father and the Son' had to do with both a general intention to save all conditionally and an absolute intention to save the elect effectually (see Calvin, #22). Without raising the question of priority (temporal or logical) over the two aspects of God's redemptive decree, both Calvin and Amyraut taught an indiscriminate dimension to the atonement as well as a particular one (see Calvin, #44, 49, 65). If this seems strangely 'out of joint' from Rainbow's perspective, facts remain facts.

There can be no doubt that Amyraut's theology of redemption was thoroughly trinitarian. From the evidence cited already, Calvin and Amyraut are in perfect harmony, despite Rainbow's attempt to argue otherwise (p. 78). It is also plain that the author often argues at the expense of key Calvin quotations. Had he been aware of Calvin's full statements on the love of God (#8, 45), he would not have denied that Calvin taught a general salvific love of God as well as a special love. When Calvin says that 'God embraces in fatherly love none but his children' (cited by Rainbow, p. 80), 'embraces' is clearly akin to 'grasps' in *Comm. 2 Pet. 3:9* (#83). This is clearly the language of efficacious love, a truth stressed by Amyraut no less than Calvin (see Armstrong, p. 199). Rainbow himself wrote unwittingly that 'The redemption which the Father effected through the Son was, then, the outworking of his special love for the elect' (p. 81, emphasis mine). Precisely. But 'special' love implies a 'general' love, which both Amyraut and Calvin saw in salvific and not merely providential terms. It is simply untrue that 'There was no trace in Calvin's theology of the doctrine attributed to him by Amyraut, that Christ came to carry out something other than the predestinating decree of God for the salvation of the elect' (p. 87).

Amyraut was right to see in Calvin a two-fold intent in the work of Christ (#12, 42) correlating with the two-fold will of God (#21, 27). Only ignorance of Calvin permits one to say otherwise. See also Comm. John 12:47 (#49); *Comm. Rom. 5:18* (#58), neither of which are cited by Rainbow. Clearly, many of Rainbow's observations fly in the face of Calvin data. Regarding his comments on assurance (p. 88), it is plain that those who hear the universal gospel are entitled to assurance when they believe (and not otherwise), since faith is evidence of election. Notwithstanding the outworking of the feodus absolutum, the gospel is presented as a conditional offer: assurance is granted to those who fulfill the condition of repentance and faith (#21, 22, 66, 74).

When Rainbow considers the doctrine of redemption in the wider context of Calvin's soteriology, he draws attention to the reformer's use of the Aristotelian device of fourfold causation (pp. 89ff). He argues that Calvin's resort to this scheme is consistent only with limited redemption. There can be no doubt that Calvin's occasional use of this amounts to a kind of *argumentum ad hominem*, designed to exclude the place of human merit and to emphasise the sovereignty of divine grace. However, Rainbow clearly overstates his case. He imagines that Calvin's stress on divine causation necessarily eliminates any conditional elements from his thought. The evidence cited above surely demonstrates that Calvin was able to live with biblical paradox in his soteriology. While he believed that the election of the Father, the mediation of the Son and the regeneration of the Holy Spirit guaranteed faith for the elect, he was frequently happy to stress the conditional duty of believing without implying a denial of the divine purpose. Calvin didn't cram every aspect of his soteriology into every salvific statement. Amyraut's theology shows the same awareness and acceptance of paradox. Again, Rainbow imagines that when 'Amyraut believed that Christ's death did not become effectual except through faith' (p. 94) he was denying the causal factors of divine grace. However Amyraut's Alençon statement corrects this misconception. Thus, when Rainbow says 'The death of Christ does not wait for faith. It generates it' (p. 95), he fails to see - by ignoring the principle of paradox in both Amyraut's and Calvin's theology - that both are true.

When Rainbow discusses the unity of the work of Christ (pp. 96ff), he again ignores the basic dualism employed by both Amyraut and Calvin. It is perfectly plain, *contra* Rainbow and Kendall, that the same dualism which applies to Christ's death also applies to his intercession. They are indeed coextensive, but in Calvin's dualistic sense (see #51). Rainbow ignores Calvin's universal intercession statement here. This does not contradict Calvin's comment elsewhere once his careful qualification is noted: 'It is likely that Christ did not pray for all without distinction, but only for the wretched populace who were carried along by thoughtless zeal, not deliberate wickedness. As there was no hope remaining for the scribes and priests, prayer for them would have had no effect' (*Comm. Luke 23: 34*). In short, Christ's prayer was otherwise 'universal'.

While Rainbow insists that the benefits of Christ's resurrection, intercession and kingly rule are confined to the elect, Calvin's dualism is evident in the very extracts cited. '...it was *especially* for the benefit of his church that he rose again,...' (p. 98, emphasis mine). 'So then, the kingdom of Christ extends, no doubt, to *all* men; *but* it brings salvation to none but the elect,...' (p. 99, emphases mine). Since Calvin wrote dualistically on such matters, is it any wonder that he viewed redemption as he did? What Rainbow mistakenly regards as a soteriological scheme confined to the elect is nothing else than the special, effectual application of an otherwise general provision of grace. Contrary to Rainbow's reflections on Amyraut (pp. 103f), the dualism of the 'Amyraut thesis' had its very origin in Calvin!

Whether Rainbow likes it or not, Calvin's commitment to the concept of penal substitution did not involve a Gottschalkian and Bezan theory of satisfaction and limited redemption. He never subscribed to the 'double payment' doctrine of Beza. Rightly or wrongly, Calvin even declares that unbelievers are 'doubly culpable' for rejecting salvation. He clearly did not take up the commercialistic ideas of Anselm as Rainbow virtually admits (p. 109; see also Calvin, #11, 17, 18, 20, 77).

Rainbow attempts to prove that Calvin taught limited redemption by citing 'Christ died for the elect' type of statements (pp. 110ff). Of course there are many, but such statements are no threat to Amyraut. However, the author's thesis really demands 'Christ died for the elect alone' statements, of which there are none. Indeed, it is easy to refute the thesis by reading further on! For instance, Rainbow cites *Comm. 2 Cor. 6:2*, 'The Father [appointed] the Son a leader for the gathering of the Church...' In the next paragraph, Calvin - with obvious evangelistic intent - also wrote: '...when Christ appeared, salvation was sent to the whole world, so now it is sent to us every day, when we are made partakers of the Gospel'. Similarly, Rainbow's citing of *Comm. Eph. 1:11* may be balanced by *Sermons* on *Ephesians*, p. 55 (#67). Likewise the citation from Calvin's sermon on Matthew 27:45-54 (p. 114) is complemented by *Comm. Matt. 26:1-2* (#28). All this surely points in an Amyraldian rather than a limited redemption direction.

Rainbow's contention that Calvin actually denied universal redemption largely depends on the questionable linguistic devices discussed earlier. Predictably the author appeals first to the Heshusius statement I have dealt with elsewhere (*Calvinus*: introduction). Suffice to say here that Calvin did not say 'Christ did not die for the wicked' (p. 119). He asked 'how the wicked can eat the flesh of Christ which was not crucified for them, etc?' In other words, his query has more to do with the absurdities of consubstantiation than the extent of the atonement.

Rainbow's citations at pp. 120-24 do not help his case: they fit quite comfortably into Amyraut's theology of limited efficacious redemption. In *Comm. John 12: 32*, the moderating influence of Chrysostom on a strictly Augustinian exegesis is noteworthy. From other Calvin statements ignored by Rainbow, notably *Comm. John 3:16* (#45, 57) and *Comm. Rom. 5:18* (#58), it is absurdly false to claim that for Calvin 'the human race' is 'the assembly of the elect from every kind of humanity' (p. 123). Neither did he subscribe to the Augustinian 'two worlds' concept. Clearly, the elect are saved from the human race, even if they may be regarded thereafter as a 'new humanity'.

These latter observations also apply to Rainbow's treatment of Calvin's comments on Col. 1:20 and John 11:51. Whereas the 'all' of Col. 1:20 are those efficaciously redeemed, Calvin still affirmed a wider redemptive provision in *Comm. Col. 1:14* (#70). Calvin uses John 11:51 in *Eternal Predestination*, p. 148 (#85) where he also argues that benefits received by the elect are nonetheless offered to all on the basis of a universal redemption. Clearly the elect are gathered from the world. Calvin's distinction between benefits offered to all but received by some is crucial for a right understanding of *Comm. 1 John 2:2*. Although he might have viewed John's statement in a natural universal sense, Calvin's concern to combat the theory of an absolute universalism (including the reprobate and Satan) led him to expound the verse in terms of efficacious extent: 'the design of John was no other than to make this benefit (or blessing) common to the whole church'. However, Calvin's similar exegesis of 1 John 2:2 in the *Eternal Predestination* passage cited above (#85) is followed by the affirmation that such redemptive benefits are nonetheless offered to all on the basis of a universal redemption. Unfortunately, Rainbow obscures this fact, having deleted this key passage from his quotation (p. 131).

Rainbow is clearly in difficulties. Believing that Calvin was strictly Augustinian regarding a single divine intention to save the elect, he says 'then it is pointless to think of the death of Christ in any other way' (p. 132). Thus, 'there are not two divine saving wills, one universal and one particular...' (p. 133). However, when confronted by Calvin's ubiquitous universalism later in the book, he is forced to admit - before hastening to restate his equally ubiquitous concern to separate Calvin from Amyraut - that 'Calvin clearly articulated a universal saving will of God that was conditional on faith...' (p. 149).

As I have shown, Rainbow's anti-Amyraldian observations rest on inadequate data. Another case in point is his discussion of the sufficiency-efficiency distinction (pp. 133-4) touched on above. While it is true that Calvin denied its relevance to 1 John 2:2, he was happy to use it elsewhere, albeit occasionally (see #18, 19, 42). Rainbow's reference to Zacharias Ursinus (1534-83) is also misleading since Ursinus (or rather his pupil David Pareus (1548-1622) who completed Ursinus' commentary on the *Heidelberg Catechism*) clearly anticipated Amyraut's understanding of the sufficiency-efficiency distinction: '[Christ] died for all, in respect to the sufficiency of his ransom; and for the faithful alone in respect of the efficacy of the same, so also he willed to die for all in general, as touching the sufficiency of his merit...But he willed to die for the elect alone as touching the efficacy of his death' (*Commentary on the Heidelberg Catechism*, tr. G. W. Williard, 1852, p. 223, given in my *Atonement and Justification*, p. 75). Compared with the high orthodox divines of Dordt (for some agreed with Pareus' view), it is clearly arguable that Calvin - like John Cameron (1580-1625) and his pupil Amyraut - held this more 'ample' view of the distinction (see Armstrong, p. 59). Rainbow's quotation of Calvin's reply to Pighius is also misleading. By deleting a significant portion, he hides Calvin's proto-Amyraldian sentiments from view (see #63).

Contrary to Rainbow's claim, it should now be clear that Calvin was not strictly Augustinian in his understanding of 1 Tim. 2:4-6, notwithstanding his 'universalism of kinds' exegesis. Calvin did not follow Augustine in his fundamental approach to the passage. Unlike Augustine, Calvin insisted that Paul had God's revealed will rather than the absolute will in mind. Rainbow ignores a key passage from *Eternal Predestination* (#72), where Calvin insists Paul means 'not individuals of nations' but 'nations of individuals'. In short, since the revealed will is the issue, individuals of each class are mercifully invited to salvation through the external preaching of the Gospel. From this perspective, the atonement is relevant to every member of every class. Contrary to the author's criticism of Amyraut (p. 143), it is plain that the Saumur professor was a more careful expositor of Calvin's thought than he is. He and many others have failed to see the significance of Calvin's unique exegesis of 1 Tim. 2:4-6. One is entitled to ask, why then did Calvin resort to a 'universalism of kinds' at all? Simply because the Apostle was not naming particular kings and rulers. However the 'hope of salvation' was open to any and every king as much as to any and every private person who hears the Gospel. Whether they are elect doesn't come into the picture at this stage. As if to exploit Calvin for his own ends, Rainbow cites Calvin's seeming reluctance to evangelize the Turks (p. 139). Of course, Calvin is commenting on the mystery of providence - the outworking of God's secret will. Perhaps the reformer wasn't always clear what foot to stand on, but on this subject, Calvin was as universalist as ever: 'Behold the Turks, which cast away the grace which was purchased for all the world by Jesus Christ: the Jews do the like...' (*Sermons on Timothy and Titus*, p. 177).

Rainbow is clearly not quite comfortable in handling Calvin's numerous universalist statements. His anxiety to drive a wedge between Calvin and Amyraut is most apparent here. After conceding the strong dualistic similarities between Calvin and Amyraut, he still insists that 'Calvin's doctrine of the universal offer did not, Amyraut's analysis notwithstanding, imply universal redemption' (p. 151). One wonders why Calvin's comments on John 1:29 (#44), John 3:16 (#45, 57), Rom. 5:18 (#58) and Gal. 5:12 (#65) are not cited in Rainbow's 'short representative sample' (pp. 153f)? Had they been, his case would surely have collapsed at a glance.

Rainbow's citation of *Comm. John 1: 49* (p. 155) lends further weight to the very dualism Amyraut found in Calvin. Recognising the unity of the Scriptures, Calvin clearly saw New Testament soteriological antecedents in the Old Testament. The eternal Christ was now king over the whole world as he had been over Israel of old. While the sacrificial system provided redemption for every Israelite throughout the nation's history, not all were effectually saved for not all were elect (Rom. 9: 6). Thus redemption was 'sufficient for all but efficient for the elect' (Isa. 53: 1, 6, 12). As the high priest on the Day of Atonement represented all the tribes of Israel, so Christ now represents all the nations of the world (see Calvin, #2, 4, 76, 78). The New Testament Gospel is simply an internationalization of the Old Testament Gospel. The OT 'universalism of tribes' symbolized by the ephod of the high priest emerges as the NT 'universalism of nations'. In both cases, redemptive provision is offered to individual members of each tribe and nation even if many reject it (see Calvin, #18). Limited redemptionists are thus confronted by the problem of apostasy within the redeemed community: not all Israel were saved though they were - in a sense - redeemed. Calvin's important comments on 2 Pet. 2:1 (#82) - not cited by Rainbow - and Jude 4 (#87) are relevant at this point.

This brings us to Rainbow's discussion of the final group of Calvin statements, those implying that souls perish for whom Christ died (pp. 159ff). We are told that this, the 'best evidence on the side of the Amyraut thesis' was 'hardly tapped by Amyraut or his recent sympathizers' (p. 159). Rainbow's impressive list of Calvin statements is far more extensive than the universal statements (pp. 160-2; see #12, 54, 55, 68, 79, 82, 87). In order to keep his precarious thesis afloat, the author maintains that Calvin's teaching relates not to soteriology but to pastoral care. The various gyrations made by the author to establish his case are not impressive. We are asked to believe, assuming Calvin was a limited redemptionist, that he never saw the relevant NT texts as threats to his soteriology. One question immediately exposes the fatal flaw in Rainbow's thesis: why in all these statements on pastoral care does Calvin speak soteriologically? Indeed, in every one of them, redemption is the key thought and primary motivation. Is it remotely possible to imagine that Calvin, who became a theologian in order to be a pastor, could ever employ a practical, working assumption without a dogmatic basis? To say Calvin's statements have absolutely nothing to do with the extent of the atonement is really to read them blindfolded. Rainbow's further concession that Calvin did teach a 'universal saving will of God' as well as the 'elective decree of God' (p. 171) surely points to the true reason why Calvin was not troubled theologically by the issues involved. The death of Christ can be, and often is, negated, ruined and wasted by man with respect to its 'potential' redemptive provision but not according to its 'kinetic', efficacious impact on the elect. In pastoral and evangelistic activity, Calvin obviously taught that God's gracious revealed will is frustrated time and time again but that the elective will ensured the infallible redemption of the true church (see #48, 51, 52, 83). In other words, the relevant NT texts involved no denial of the doctrine of limited efficacious redemption. Such was the authentic doctrine of Calvin. It was also the doctrine of Amyraut.

One can only conclude that the anti-Amyraldian interpretation of Calvin does not stand up under scrutiny (to invert Rainbow's words, p. 175). The answer to his own question 'why does the doctrine of limited redemption not appear clearly in the *Institutes*?' can only be: 'The author never believed it'. Only by flying in the face of clear evidence can Dr Rainbow insist that 'Limited redemption was the doctrine of Calvin' (p. 180). Only by using forced inference and prejudiced interpretation can Amyraut's claim to be a faithful disciple of Calvin be falsified. Indeed, Calvin was a Calvinist, as Dr Rainbow soundly affirms. Not 'two Calvins' as he contemptuously styles Amyraut's hero (p. 158), but a dualistic Calvin to be sure. It is perhaps tragic that after the reformer's death, the Reformed world saw a floodtide of theologians who were the real pseudo-Calvinists. Amyraut, like a Reformed Noah, kept the dualistic *feodus gratiae* afloat. While Dr Rainbow's book is certainly colourful and incisive it failed to convince. So having read what is probably the most thorough attempted refutation of Amyraut to date, the author of this critique remains as decided an Amyraldian Calvinist as ever.

Postscript: Consistent with his self-contradictory case *Calvin and the Calvinists* (Banner of Truth, 1982), which I reviewed accordingly in the *Evangelical Times* (October, 1982), Paul Helm commended Dr Rainbow's book with a highly predictable review (see *The Banner of Truth*, January, 1993). Helm expressed the hope that Rainbow's book would end the 'paper chase' over Calvin's view of the atonement. My critique of Rainbow demonstrates why Helm's conclusion was merely wishful thinking. It is to be regretted that the 'Calvin taught limited atonement' viewpoint was not nipped in the bud when it emerged on the eve of the 'Owenite revival' in the 1950s. At the 1953 IVF Tyndale Fellowship Conference, the Barthian J. B. Torrance rightly argued 'that Calvin never allowed his doctrine of election to lead to a doctrine of limited atonement. He was immediately challenged by John Murray, who asserted that Calvin did teach that Christ died only for the elect. But since he could not quote Calvin to that effect, Murray retreated to the ground that the doctrine was implicit in Calvin's thought. James Torrance quoted Calvin's sermon on 1Timothy 2: 4 [*Calvinus*, #73] and 2 Peter 2: 1 [*Calvinus*, #82]. James Packer then took up the cudgels, asking whether Christ made our salvation actual or possible. When Torrance said 'actual' he then pressed upon him the logical alternatives of universalism or limited atonement. The arguments from history and exegesis having made no headway, recourse was made to logic' (T. A. Noble, *Tyndale House and Fellowship: The First Sixty Years*, IVP, 2006, 76). Of course, his theological allegiance having switched from Baxter - the subject of his Oxford D. Phil thesis (1954) - to Owen, Packer had rigged the question. The correct 'authentic Calvinist' answer was that since Christ's death made salvation conditionally *applicable* to all though absolutely *applied* to the elect, it was both 'possible' for all and 'actual' for some.

Appendix III

I

See Iain H. Murray, 'Calvin and the Atonement' (*The Banner of Truth*, November 1996, pp. 17-20).

Committed to the high orthodoxy of John Owen, the Revd Iain Murray's review of *Calvinus* was predictable. It merely recycles conventional anti-Amyraldian propaganda. Indeed, it shows only a superficial attempt to evaluate the Calvin evidence on which Amyraut's case was based. Since I anticipated and answered all Mr Murray's criticisms, those who take the trouble to study the evidence objectively will rapidly perceive how flawed and inadequate his response is. His disclaimer that the definition of 'authentic Calvinism' is 'a question of little consequence' (p. 20) is not very convincing, since he insists on rescuing Calvin from the imputation of Amyraldianism (pp. 18, 19). Of course, Mr Murray is a victim of the high-orthodox Owenite neurosis that Amyraldianism involves compromise with Arminian error. Thus when he compares the Arminian and Amyraldian versions of the universal and particular features of the gospel, he cannot avoid aligning Amyraldianism with the Arminian view of universal expiation (p. 17). The fact remains that Amyraut derived his distinctives from Calvin and - more importantly - the Bible.

Mr Murray's failure to consider the historical case made by *Calvinus* is not impressive - especially for one who claims to be a historian. His appeal to what he calls 'traditional reformed theology' ignores the fact that Amyraut's position had a precedent in the early Reformed confessions (including the Canons of Dordt) as well as in Calvin. On the subject of the atonement, the *Heidelberg Catechism* (1563), Q. 37, was expounded by its author Dr Zacharias Ursinus using the very 'combination of the universal with the particular' Murray attributes to Amyraut (p. 18). From this historical perspective, Murray's so-called 'traditional reformed theology' was a novelty of the post-Dordt era. His statement that 'God has not chosen to explain how salvation is offered to those for whom it has not been obtained' (p. 18) would have been dismissed as ludicrous by late sixteenth-century Reformed theologians. Even Dr William Twisse, the first prolocutor of the Westminster Assembly could write that 'everyone who hears the gospel (without distinction between elect and reprobate) is bound to believe that Christ has died for him, so far as to procure both the pardon of his sins and the salvation of his soul, in case he believes and repents'. Such is the obvious drift of the New Testament rightly recognised by first and second generation Calvinists. Murray's difficulties derive from erroneous scholastic departures from an earlier and more biblically balanced Calvinism. One wonders what more Calvin should have said to persuade Murray that he taught (besides its certain efficacy for the elect) 'a conditional, hypothetical redemption' for all. The conclusion is obvious: the *Calvinus* evidence has been largely dismissed.

One is encouraged that Mr Murray grants some concessions, a fact which might not please his Owenite friends. Indeed, regarding the view that God still desires the salvation of those whom he decrees finally not to save, Amyraut is a disciple of Calvin (p. 18). Now, if Murray can see this in Calvin, how can he miss the correlative truth that Calvin also taught 'an atonement for all conditionally' (p. 19)? How can he also deny that Calvin taught 'the idea of an atonement decreed for those to whom it is never applied' (p. 19)? The simple truth is that he is unwilling to admit the evidence. At the risk of being tedious, I quote Calvin again: 'The sacrifice [of Christ] was ordained by the eternal decree of God, to expiate the sins of the world' (#31). 'God commends to us the salvation of all men without exception, even as Christ suffered for the sins of the whole world' (#65). 'Although Christ suffered for the sins of the world, and is offered by the goodness of God without distinction to all men, yet not all receive him' (#58). 'God receiveth us to mercy...upon condition that we return unto God' (#74). 'It is of course certain that not all enjoy the fruits of Christ's death, but this happens because their unbelief hinders them' (#77). What could be clearer?

Anxious to distance Calvin from Amyraut, Mr Murray seeks to refute the latter's view of the divine decree without implicating the former. But clearly, Amyraut derived his 'double decree' doctrine from Calvin (see *Calvinus*, #21, 22, 27, 71-3, 83). Instead of honestly criticising Calvin as well, Murray targets Amyraut by appealing to George Smeaton's criticism of the Amyraldian position (p. 19). We are told that the general and special aspects of the decree are 'conflicting', 'discordant' and 'incoherent' (p.19), and that Amyraldianism arises from 'confused thought' (p. 20). Such language reveals the incipient rationalism of Smeaton, Murray and others of the Owenite school. Now, unlike Calvin and Amyraut, their rationalist critics are unhappy with paradox. But the conditional and absolute elements in the decree are at worst paradoxical and at best complementary rather than contradictory. The latter would only apply if the two elements involved two absolute divine purposes. Just as Calvin views the divine will (or decree) in a two-fold manner, so does Amyraut. However, exactly like Calvin, Amyraut is anxious to argue that this two-fold will is 'one only act of [God's] eternal and unchangeable will' (*Calvinus*, p. 29). Had Mr Murray read this, he would not have cited John Murray's perfectly acceptable view of the divine will as a futile device to separate Calvin from Amyraut (p. 19).

Mr Murray's unscholarly refusal to discuss the details of the debate is his undoing. His attempt to denigrate my supposed 'mastery of Calvin' (p. 19) unhappily backfires. I am accused of citing Calvin's Commentary on 1 Timothy 2: 4-6 to the neglect of the Reformer's Sermons on the same passage, as if the two expositions conflict. However, the sermons in question are amply quoted in *Calvinus* (#73). Contrary to Murray's rather careless observation, they make the identical point to the Commentary that, in Calvin's view, Paul is not discussing the elective, efficacious will of God as Owen was to maintain. While I do not claim an omniscient mastery of Calvin's writings, I do understand him accurately in this instance, as any careful reader may verify. As for Mr Murray, a slightly more scholarly approach would have been less embarrassing for him; his misinformation does him no credit. Indeed, his patronizing review lacks integrity.

I emphatically do believe 'that a man cannot be a true Calvinist if he fails to believe with Amyraut in a redemption which is both universal and particular' (p. 20). According to authentic Calvinism, the entire Bible presents God's dealings with mankind in both conditional and absolute terms. There clearly is potentiality and actuality in the death of Christ. By itself, it saves no one without the application of the Holy Spirit. Even the elect are not actually saved until the benefits of the atonement are applied to them, notwithstanding God's eternal purpose to do so. Contrary to men of Mr Murray's stamp, Calvin was quite clear about this (see *Calvinus*, #7). As for the oft-lamented dangers of Amyraldianism, it no more inclines towards Arminianism than Owenism does towards hypercalvinism. It is an ungracious and fallacious slur to imply that the gospel is less safe with Amyraldians than with Mr Murray and his friends. Only a combination of arrogance and ignorance can deny that 'the Puritans and their successors' included 'authentic' as well as 'pseudo-Calvinists' like the Revd Iain Murray.

II

See Iain H. Murray, *The Old Evangelicalism: Old Truths for a New Awakening* (Banner of Truth Trust, Edinburgh, 2005).

On a personal and pastoral level, I share most of the concerns expressed by the author in this book. In content and tone, there is much to applaud, especially Mr Murray's opposition to hypercalvinism. In this respect, a healthy drop of Wesleyan spirit (p. 128) adds welcome fuel to his argument. However, from an academic perspective, his discussion and supporting citations leave much to be desired. Indeed, in his 'cherry-picking' approach, he stretches academic charity beyond tolerable limits. He is either ignorant of what he ought to know, or he deliberately suppresses information he disapproves of. To give him his due, Mr Murray obviously wishes to approach the outer limits of the biblically permissible - but without infringing 'confessional correctness' (p. 106). Sadly, this appears to be his dominant doctrinal concern, an emphasis wedded to the dubious assumption that *Westminster Confession* orthodoxy and biblical fidelity mean the same thing. Without identifying the Amyraldian synthesis as such, the author attempts to dismiss the 'double reference' view of the atonement from his highly defective discussion. That said, his entire treatment places considerable strain on his fundamental 'Owenite' agenda.

The reader may be forgiven for assuming that all Mr Murray's authorities endorse his 'definite (or properly 'exclusively-limited') atonement' thesis (p. 106). However, this is simply not the case. Indeed, the vast majority of them expressed a quasi-Amyraldian viewpoint. Even Augustine of Hippo, whose statement provides Mr Murray's 'The Cross - The Pulpit of God's Love' chapter heading, was a 'proto-Amyraldian' (see my 'Reply 6' to Roger Nicole - including Baxter's comment - in Appendix I, p. 40). Even John Murray, for all his *WCF* particularism grants that there is a sense in which 'Christ died for non-elect persons' (*Collected Writings*, i. 68). As for Jonathan Edwards, even Mr Murray's citation (at p. 106) tends to confirm what we now know of Edwards' clear Amyraldian leanings, e.g. see his *Miscellanies* in the volume cited by Mr Murray (n. 6):

> 424. UNIVERSAL REDEMPTION. Christ did die for all in this sense, that all by his death have an opportunity of being [saved]; and he had that design in dying, that they should have that opportunity by it. For it was certainly a thing that God designed, that all men should have such an opportunity, or else they would not have it; and they have it by the death of Christ.

In this respect, in his biography of Jonathan Edwards, Murray failed to do justice to Edwards' influence on his pupil Joseph Bellamy whose avowedly Amyraldian treatise *True Religion Delineated* (1750) was launched with a preface by Edwards. Indeed, Edwards was evidently *not* satisfied with Owen's strict particularism. That said, Augustine and Edwards would undoubtedly approve of Mr Murray's own unwitting agreement with their position. To say 'the good news of a provided forgiveness is to be ... universally proclaimed' (p. 107) surely indicates a general dimension to an atonement otherwise particularly efficacious to the elect.

Notwithstanding Mr Murray's use of A. A. Hodge's dismissal of Amyraldianism in his review of *Calvinus*, his father Charles Hodge (cited by Murray, p. 109) - despite his formal rejection of the Amyraldian view - rejected strict Owenism: 'Augustinians do not deny that Christ died for all men. What they deny is that He died equally, and with the same design, for all men' (*Systematic*

Theology, 1960, ii. 558). The same may be said of Robert L. Dabney (cited on p. 113) who distanced himself from John Owen's particularism: 'I have already stated one ground for rejecting that interpretation of John 3:16, which makes 'the world' which God so loved, the elect world. ... Christ's mission to make expiation for sin is a manifestation of unspeakable benevolence to the whole world' (*Systematic Theology*, 1878, 535). Clearly, these authors step beyond the confines of *WCF* orthodoxy.

In all his quotations from John Owen (pp. 109, 113, 120-1), Murray disingenuously keeps the *Death of Death* out of sight. Thus readers are shielded from the 'limited-love-of-the-elect-world' exegesis of John 3: 16 found there. In this crucial respect, Owen is a total threat to Mr Murray's case for a doctrine of 'universal divine love' (p. 114). Significantly, John Calvin is Murray's ally on this specific issue (p. 112). Murray makes the same point when writing of John Wesley (see p. 161 and *Wesley and the Men who Followed,* Banner of Truth, 2003, p. 60). However, as if it would undermine his anti-Amyraldian stance, Mr Murray fails to quote even one of the numerous correlative universal atonement quotations from Calvin as found in *Calvinus*. Who can fail to see that in Calvin's thinking, God's universal love, Christ's universal atonement and the universal offer of the gospel stand together? Consistent with all he wrote on John 3: 16, Calvin consequently wrote thus on Romans 5: 18:

> Paul makes grace common to all, not because it in fact extends to all, but because it is offered to all. Although Christ suffered for the sins of the world, and is offered by the goodness of God without distinction to all men, yet not all receive him' (*Calvinus*, #58).

As I have written elsewhere, 'Even John Owen (Thrussington) concludes from 'this sentence that Calvin held general redemption' (see the Calvin Translation Society edition of Calvin's *Commentary on Romans*, p. 212). Roger Nicole admits that 'the passage ... comes perhaps closest to providing support for Amyraut's thesis' (*Moyse Amyraut ... and the Controversy on Universal Grace,* Harvard PhD thesis, 1966, 83). Is this the reason why Mr Murray cherry-picks as he does?

Consistent with his Owenite fixation, i. e. 'election' and 'redemption' are strictly co-extensive, Murray denies that his 'general and special love' distinction has any bearing on a 'particular and universal' view of the atonement (p. 117). Persisting with his dogma that Christ 'did not represent in his sufferings' any but the elect, Murray is incapable of grasping what John Calvin and others consider as biblically obvious. Professor Paul Helm shares Mr Murray's position (see his review of my *Amyraut Affirmed (2004)* in *Evangelicals Now*, November, 2004). Nigel Westhead's perceptive criticism of Helm is applicable to Murray:

> In my view however it would be quite reasonable *prima facie* to expect Calvin to offer the Gospel to all on the basis of an atonement made for all. One would not have expected an integrated thinker like Calvin to offer something to people that was not in actual fact available to them. In fact this is what we find on careful reading of some Calvin quotes that Dr Clifford cites. From his sermons on Isaiah 53 for example, quoted in *Amyraut Affirmed* (p. 33), Calvin, after quoting Jn. 3: 16 explains the basis upon which the 'whosoever' rests. It is because 'Our Lord Jesus suffered for *all* and there is neither great nor small who is not inexcusable today.... how will they excuse their ingratitude in not receiving *the blessing* in which they could share by faith?' (emphases mine). It is not only that the *message* is for all, but that it is so because the *sufferings* of Christ are for all. The co-ordinate and co-extensiveness of offering and suffering are clear in Calvin's comments on Romans 5: 18. '... Christ *suffered for* the sins of the world, and is *offered* by the goodness of God without distinction to all men...' Again in his

comments on 2 Corinthians 5 (*Amyraut Affirmed*, p. 35), Calvin states, '... God was in Christ … reconciling the world [note the universality for Calvin is not only at the point *of application*, but also at the point of *accomplishment*] … *as* he once suffered, *so* now he offers the fruit of his sufferings to us through the Gospel... '[note again the coterminous nature of suffering and offering] (A. C. Clifford, *Spotlight on Scholastics: Clarifying Calvinism - Responses to Carl Trueman, Richard Muller and Paul Helm*, 2005, pp. 8-9).

The glaring defects of Mr Murray's case are evident when we examine his other authorities. For instance, on the issue of God's two-fold will, he sympathetically cites the late Puritan John Howe (p. 117). Yet Howe was an Amyraldian friend of Baxter (see my 'Introduction' to John Davenant's *Dissertation on the Death of Christ*, 2006, p. xvii). John Bunyan is cited for proclaiming God's loving universal offers of mercy, yet he also declared:

'Christ died for all. ... for if those that perish in the days of the gospel, shall have, at least, their damnation heightened, because they have neglected and refused to receive the gospel, it must needs be that the gospel was with all faithfulness to be tendered unto them; the which it could not be, unless the death of Christ did extend itself unto them; John 3: 16. Heb.2: 3. for the offer of the gospel cannot with God's allowance, be offered any further than the death of Jesus Christ doth go' (*Reprobation Asserted* in *The Works of John Bunyan*, ed. George Offor (1855), ii. 348).

Mr Murray's repeated appeals to Thomas Chalmers (pp. 104, 117, 131) are especially glaring examples of his cherry-picking approach. When he says that Chalmers 'believed in particular redemption' on the basis of his rejection of Thomas Erskine's doctrine of universal pardon (p. 117), he creates the impression that Chalmers shared Murray's 'Owenite' stance. Yet Chalmers cannot be bracketed with his fellow Scot Robert S. Candlish whose muddled particularism (p. 122) is used by Murray as a springboard to assert that 'any making of saving faith to rest on a statement that 'Christ has died for you' is dangerously wrong' (p. 123). For this extraordinary opinion, Mr Murray appeals to C. H. Spurgeon who was concerned to define correctly the 'object of faith': 'you may believe that Jesus Christ died for you, and may believe what is not true; you may believe that which will bring you no sort of good whatever. ... Do not get that into your head, or it will ruin you' (p. 123). Even if we may grant that Spurgeon is (rather clumsily) warning against the danger of mere head knowledge rather than personal 'trust', the thrust of his argument is at least bizarre and at worst appallingly anti-evangelical. Indeed, since sinners are called to place their trust in Christ, are they not to come to Christ as 'Christ crucified'? Does He not call us to Himself on the basis of His available propitiation, a reality to be known, declared and offered *prior* to believing?

Thomas Chalmers had no doubts on this score: 'I do not object, you will observe, to the object of their faith being in this particular form, that He died for my sins - as I hold that the precious terms of *all* and *any* and *whosoever* wherein the overtures of the gospel are couched, abundantly warrant this blessed appropriation' (*Institutes of Theology*, 1849, ii. 156) . Thus, in language Owen never used, Chalmers affirmed:

'If Christ died only for the elect, and not for all', then ministers 'are puzzled to understand how they should proceed with the calls and invitations of the gospel. ... Now for the specific end of conversion, the available scripture is not that Christ laid down His life for the sheep, but that Christ is set forth a propitiation for the sins of the world. It is not because I know myself to be one of the sheep, or one of the elect, but because I know myself to be one of the world, that I take to myself the calls and promises of the New Testament' (*Institutes of Theology*, ii. 403, 406).

Chalmers was convinced on purely biblical rather than confessional grounds. Indeed, Mr Murray's assumption that 'what Scripture asserts' (pp. 118, 124) and 'what the *Westminster Confession* asserts' are really equivalent, is a view Chalmers did not share. Indeed, he rejected the mentality of 'stour orthodox folk just over-ready to stretch the Bible to square with their Catechism: ... but what I say is, do not let that wretched mutilated thing come between me and the Bible' (W. Hanna, *Memoirs of Thomas Chalmers*, 1854, ii. 729). Contrary to Mr Murray's view, 'much error' arises when Scripture is filtered through *WCF* ultra-orthodoxy. This is the major defect of Mr Murray's whole case. Hence Richard Baxter speaks for all the authorities misrepresented by Mr Murray:

> 'When God saith so expressly that Christ died for all [2 Cor. 5: 14-15], and tasted death for every man [Heb. 2: 9], and is the ransom for all [1 Tim. 2: 6], and the propitiation for the sins of the whole world [1 Jn. 2: 2], it beseems every Christian rather to explain in what sense Christ died for all, than flatly to deny it' (*The Universal Redemption of Mankind*, 1694, p. 286).

Since he *does* profess a desire to follow the Scriptures, why then does Mr Murray not adopt Baxter's truly scriptural approach? His dismissal of 'explanations of the extent of the atonement' (p. 124) is an attempt to avoid the fact that the very men he appeals to provided 'explanations' at odds with his own. Indeed, does he not embrace and affirm John Owen's 'explanation of the limited extent of the atonement'? In addition, it is simply not helpful to indulge in pietistic blackmail in order to shield his highly dubious position from scrutiny. Warning against 'God-dishonouring debate' (p. 127) has no integrity unless the 'warner' himself handles evidence honourably. However, in Mr Murray's case, it sounds like a rhetorical device to stifle discussion about the heart of the Gospel.

Mr Murray's conclusion perpetuates to the last the misinformation he presents to the reader. Here he is at odds with works published by his own organisation - the Banner of Truth Trust. Not to mention J. C. Ryle's *Expository Thoughts on John's Gospel* (a thoroughly *Amyraldian* exposition), a notable example is *The Atonement Controversy in Welsh Theological Literature and Debate, 1707-1841* by Owen Thomas, tr. by John Aaron (2002). Concerned to learn lessons about the dangers of theoretical rather than practical theological discussion (pp. 125-7), Mr Murray - like the book's translator - is opposed to the author's chief concern - to assert the true doctrine of the extent of the atonement. As a true 'son' of Thomas Chalmers, Owen Thomas and many of his brethren were convinced that the scholastic 'Owenite' doctrine of limited atonement involved an 'unscriptural limitation' (p. 323) which discouraged active and compassionate evangelism (*note*: unlike Richard Baxter, John Owen never knew of anyone converted under his ministry - see *The Works of John Owen*, ed. W. H. Goold, 1967 rep., viii, p. viii).

Thomas and his friends were persuaded that Article 18 of the Calvinistic Methodist *Confession of Faith* (1823) was 'wise above what is written' (p. 323). Indeed, this article *Of Redemption* is more 'particular' than the *Westminster Confession of Faith* equivalent (see my *Atonement and Justification*, 1990/2002, p. 89). These arguments had significant effect. In 1874, the year Thomas's book was published, the General Assembly of the denomination (Carmarthen, 1874; Portmadoc, 1875) modified the interpretation of the article with an appendix stressing the universal sufficiency of the atonement (p. 324). In short, the whole controversy concerned the true character of Calvinism. Despite Mr Murray's stance and the translator's criticisms, Owen Thomas had done his homework well. He was thoroughly aware that John Calvin and many other reformers both Continental and British did not teach the doctrine of limited atonement (p. 123) and that the Canons of Dort maintain a universal dimension in the atonement (p. 124). The first of these accurate and well-established observations is dismissed with a doubtful two-fold appeal to the highly debateable studies of Robert A. Peterson and Paul Helm (pp. 123, 126). In all this highly biased discussion, the translator fails to perceive the integrity and accuracy of the author's case. The former's reference to 'classical Reformed teaching' (p. xxxiii) is question begging. By blaming 'moderate Calvinism' as 'Calvinism in decay' (p. xxxii), Aaron is effectively saying that 'Calvin's Calvinism' is dangerous!

The simple fact is that Owen Thomas and his friends saw the need to 'moderate' the 'ultra-Calvinism' of the day in order to return to a Bible-based 'Authentic Calvinism'. One may say that they sought to rescue the denomination from 'Owenistic Methodism' and to be true to correctly-defined 'Calvinistic Methodism'. In this respect, contrary to the standpoint of both translator and publisher, the author produced one of the most praise-worthy and illuminating studies in historical theology ever written. Indeed, the historical details are very revealing. After reactionary 'Owenite' John Elias' anger at an earlier meeting in Bala, the affirmation of 'true Calvinism' brought tears of joy and ecstatic 'Amens' at the Caernarvon Association of September 1828 (pp. 329-30).

In relation to Mr Murray's remarks about Dr D. Martyn Lloyd-Jones' position (p. 124), both translator and publisher (twice on the dust jacket) give a prominent profile to the highly-positive verdict on the book by Dr Lloyd-Jones. Insisting that the work was 'important to the whole question of a right preaching of Christ and the atonement', we are told that 'It would not be too much to say that [Dr Lloyd-Jones'] own gospel preaching was directly influenced by his knowledge of the pitfalls and dangers narrated by Owen Thomas' (pp. x-xi). The assumption throughout these remarks is that Dr Lloyd-Jones would have agreed with the translator's perspective on Thomas' evaluation of the controversies. Would he therefore endorse the criticisms of the translator? Probably not, to put it mildly. Two considerations justify such a verdict.

First, in 1933, the Presbyterian Church of Wales (for doubtless liberal reasons) adopted a looser attitude towards the *Confession of Faith*. Dr Lloyd-Jones showed little concern about this. In Volume 1 of his biography, Mr Murray makes no reference to this development or any thoughts Dr Lloyd-Jones might have had about it. The latter possibly welcomed the situation for thoroughly evangelistic reasons. Certainly, his *Evangelistic Sermons at Aberavon* (Banner of Truth Trust, 1983) reveal a very different emphasis from the ultra-orthodox Article 18 of the Welsh confession:

> 'But look at [Christ's] death for a moment and consider it as an expiation for the sin of the whole world. What are we told about it? Well, those sufferings were enough, according to John, for all. Listen! 'He is the propitiation for our sins; and not for ours only, but also for the sins of the whole world' (*1 Jn. 2: 2*). The whole world! ... The sins of the whole world he had borne upon Himself ' (*pp. 87-8*).

> '[If] ever you feel utterly helpless and hopeless, then turn back to Him, the Christ of the cross, with His arms outstretched, who still says: 'Look unto me and be saved, all ye ends of the earth'. It is there that the whole of humanity is focused. He is the representative of the whole of mankind. He died for all' (*p. 278*).

Second, while the Westminster Chapel years - notably the 1950s - seem to indicate a sympathy for the Banner of Truth 'Owenite' view of the atonement, the depth of Dr Lloyd-Jones' conviction on the issue is doubtful if preaching content is anything to go by. Whatever he might have said in private conversations or at conferences, limited atonement never appeared in his sermons, as Mr Murray rightly observes. During his doctoral research, Dr R. T. Kendall had a number of discussions with Dr Lloyd-Jones on John Calvin's position. Conducting his own examination of the reformer's commentaries, Dr Lloyd-Jones was obviously surprised to discover how frequently universalist Calvin's statements were. During a fortnight period, Dr Lloyd-Jones repeatedly telephoned Dr Kendall and, in excited tones said, "I've found another one!" During one discussion, he said to Dr Kendall with regard to limited atonement, "I never preached it, you know ... only once on Romans 5: 15 and I was in great difficulty when I did so." Being present, Mrs Lloyd-Jones then added, "I have never believed it and I never will!" (see my biography of Philip Doddridge, *The Good Doctor*, 2002, pp. 273-4).

These facts speak for themselves. One can only conclude that Dr Lloyd-Jones' preaching was indeed influenced by Owen Thomas' monumental work, but not in the manner assumed either by the translator or Mr Murray. Thus I conclude that 'Authentic Calvinism' provides 'gospel truth for a new awakening'. This is the truth to fill gospel preachers with love for lost sinners! Historical precedents are clear. To mention but a few locations, in Reformation Europe, Baxter's Kidderminster, Edwards' Northampton, Chalmers' Glasgow, Thomas' Wales in general and Lloyd-Jones' Aberavon in particular remind us of what could happen in our day. May God grant it, for His glory and the blessing of the world!

Postscript: Calvinus does not attempt to discuss the issues with reference to Dr John Owen's classical defence of limited atonement, *The Death of Death* (1648). For criticism of Owen, see my *Atonement and Justification: English Evangelical Theology 1640-1790 - An Evaluation* (Clarendon: Oxford, 1990 rep. 2002). These criticisms also take account of the views of Dr J. I. Packer and other advocates of Owen's theology. In his *The Claims of Truth: John Owen's Trinitarian Theology* (1998), Dr Carl Trueman challenged my critique of Owen. The title of his work is unfortunate, since his interest is not, by his own admission, 'to discover whether Owen was right or wrong' (p. ix). Indeed, in view of his concern to validate Owen's approach, the book should have been called *The Claims of Scholasticism*. Defending Owen's Trinitarian scholasticism, Trueman states that 'it would be inaccurate to interpret the Protestant notion of *sola scriptura* in such a way as to regard it as a sufficient safeguard in and of itself to safeguard the church against heresy in the seventeenth-century context. In fact, Owen's defence of orthodox Christology in the face of the radically biblicist attacks of the Socinians clearly depends upon setting the notion of *sola scriptura* and scriptural exegesis within the ongoing catholic theological tradition' (op. cit, 164). This is a clear denial of the sufficiency of Scripture, as Trueman's reviewer Ewan Wilson was quick to point out (see *English Churchman*, June 4, 1999, p. 6). Critical of eighteenth-century 'Enlightenment' heterodoxy, Dr Trueman insists that Owen's scholastic era guaranteed orthodoxy (op. cit, 93). However, considering an Enlightenment evangelical like Philip Doddridge, unlike Owen's era, Doddridge's was marked by an appeal to *data* rather than *dogma*. Whereas the 'over-orthodox' elements in Owen's theology - a kind of medieval hangover - were *dogma-driven,* Doddridge's biblical theology was *data-driven*. In short, an incipient rationalism was at work in Owen's thought. To be sure, not the kind of liberal rationalism of the eighteenth century - which Doddridge rejected - but a rationalism all the same. Of course, Dr Trueman attempts to dismiss my critique of Owen's scholastic soteriology. But, besides his failure to grasp the details of my philosophical case against Owen, his aggressive 'boxing' style is as ineffective as it is inappropriate. In short, as 'umpire' Dr Richard Muller virtually implied in an e-mail 'decision' to a friend of mine, I am 'still on my feet'! Without ever denying the scholastic element in Baxter's work (see my *Atonement and Justification*, 23, 106-7, n. 9, 143), I focused on Owen's scholasticism because, unlike Baxter's much less defective view, it had a detrimental impact on his treatment of the nature and extent of the atonement. It is undeniable that for Owen, his 'method' influenced the 'content' of his theology. In his unconvincing Westminster Conference (2006) paper, 'The Puritan Doctrine of the Atonement', Dr Garry Williams adopts a similar stance to Dr Trueman. Defending Owen's view that Christ on the cross paid the *idem* (same price) rather than the *tantundem* (an equivalent price) is a failure (as Baxter rightly pointed out) to recognise differences between Christ's actual sufferings and the eternal punishment threatening the elect, i. e. regarding their intensity and duration, etc. Only by a resort to the Aristotelian 'essence/accidents' distinction can Owen make good what is obviously not the case. Thus his commercial 'same price' concept of the atonement - on which his limited atonement dogma relies - is exploded (see my *Atonement and Justification*, 128ff).

INDEX

THE ADVANTAGES OF AMYRALDIANISM

It should now be clear that the traditional two-cornered contest between Calvinism and Arminianism is an inadequate portrayal of the issues. Not only should Amyraldianism be seen as a 'referee'; it also qualifies as the most persuasive challenger in a three-cornered contest. To make matters even clearer, the so-called Calvinist (or really *High* Calvinist) contender should really be named 'Owenism'. Accordingly we may conclude that 'Owenites' face awkward questions.

First, if a universal gospel offer is to be made, what precisely is on offer if not a universally-available redemption?

Second, if Christ died only for the elect, does it not become necessary for enquirers to discover their election *before* they come to Christ?

Third, what are the non-elect guilty of rejecting if nothing was ever offered to them?

The Amyraldian or Authentic Calvinist position possesses five advantages:

First, it provides an object lesson on how to avoid extreme reductionist hermeneutics. Theory is ever to be the servant not the master of the textual data.

Second, it enables us to accept plain statements of *Scripture* as they are without forcing them into a theological mould, *e. g.* 'world' = 'the world of the elect' (as Owen maintains). How can Owenites criticise Roman Catholics and the cults for tampering with the text when they do likewise?

Third, in keeping with God's plain declarations, it proclaims a universal compassion for the world without unwarranted restrictions. Thus the Owenite tendency to produce clinically-clear heads and callously-cramped hearts is reduced. Sadly, not all Owenites are like Whitefield and Spurgeon whose compassion arguably exceeded their creed.

Fourth, it is, in the best biblical sense, conciliatory. Significantly, Ralph Wardlaw considered that High Calvinism provided too easy an excuse for the Arminians to reject true Calvinism.

Fifth, without prying into the profundities and complexities of God's inscrutable sovereign purposes, it enables us to pursue an uninhibited mission of mercy to a lost world. We leave the results to God. While faith is evidence of election, present unbelief is not necessarily proof of non-election. There is always hope for everyone we proclaim Christ to.

Review Extracts

This book reflects the author's conclusions about Calvinism through his doctoral studies. He explores the hotly-debated issue of whether Calvin taught limited atonement. In the light of this, he examines the validity of interpretations of Calvinism made by subsequent theologians, particularly that of the French pastor Moïse Amyraut (1596-1664). ... After the introduction comes the focal point of the book: a selection of 90 extracts from the writings of John Calvin, directly expounding his views on the extent of the atonement. It is wonderful to have set before you a collection of quotations from Calvin's writings on this subject, which allow the reformer to speak for himself. This whole section is written without comment, leaving the reader to decide where Calvin really stood. ... Whatever one's opinions about 'authentic Calvinism', one would have to admit that Dr Clifford writes authoritatively and convincingly on a subject with which he is thoroughly acquainted and has extensively researched. ... [The] content is thought-provoking and stimulating, and challenging reading, especially for all who claim to be 'authentic' Calvinists!

KATHY CHILDRESS, *Evangelicals Now*

According to God's revealed will or intention the death of Christ is universal in its scope, but conditional upon the human response; according to his secret will or decree it is restricted in its scope but absolute and unconditional. Thus Calvin affirms both a conditional salvation made available to all and an efficacious, unconditional salvation given to the elect alone. It is this antinomy the author claims, rightly in my view, that makes sense of the diverse statements that Calvin makes on the subject. ... The debate about Calvin's teaching on the intent of the atonement looks set to run and run. Those who in future turn their minds to it will not be able to ignore this volume and will especially be grateful for the opportunity to review the wide range of Calvin material which is gathered together in the core of the book.

TONY LANE, *Evangelical Quarterly*

The great value of the book is the way in which the overall argument is related to Calvin's writings. ... Some authors give only sections of what Calvin wrote, some are historically selective, others give only one emphasis and leave the drift of the whole for the reader to search out. The author has done a fine job in rectifying that problem by presenting his arguments holistically. ... It must be said, and it is inevitably so, that the arguments are often subtle, all are closely argued, and at times, some can be philosophically quite sophisticated. ... However, despite the nature of the discussion, and the enormous literature generated, this book is a model of clarity and perspicacious argumentation. It is demanding, by its nature, but careful and diligent reading will give even the near novice a fine introduction to the whole issue. It is a valuable work in the continuing debate. Whether or not it will fulfil the author's wish that these issues 'will now be settled once and for all' remains to be seen, but it will deserve a serious reply from opponents. If Dr Kendall set the cat amongst the pigeons then Dr Clifford continues to rattle the reformed cage. Let the reader read and discern.

JOHN F. DUNN, *English Churchman*

Dr Clifford's scholarship is undoubtedly detailed, but his hope of settling the controversies in this volume presumably depends on the assumption that readers will have perused his more detailed study on Atonement and Justification. ... Note: 1996 is the 400th anniversary of the birth of Moïse Amyraut, whose authentic Calvinist credentials Clifford is anxious to reassert in this piece.

STEPHEN WILLIAMS, *Themelios*

This is an unusual book but it debates an all-too-familiar field. ... Clifford's claim that Calvin makes universal-sounding statements too strong to reconcile with Owen's approach seems formidable. Equally it suggests that whilst Calvin's work predates the classical differences between parties in the Reformed tradition, the subject was not quite as alien to the great Reformer as we might think. A surprising side benefit of the study also shows that Calvin was a missionary at heart and advocated personal evangelism. ... The author supplies a spirited introduction defending Amyraut and his successors, who challenged the seventeenth-century Calvinist 'high orthodoxy' with its belief in limited atonement. It is some time since Amyraut found an advocate, but the case presented here is more than worthy of such a distinguished figure. The argument will certainly rumble on yet but all parties will have to take account of this little but forceful book.

ROY KEARSLEY, *Scottish Bulletin of Evangelical Theology*